An MSNBC, FOX News, and CNN Education: Words and Terms for the Educated and Uneducated used by Cuomo, Cooper, D. Lemon, and More

Frank Palacio

"An MSNBC, FOX News, and CNN Education: Words and Terms for the Educated and Uneducated used by Cuomo, Cooper, D. Lemon, and More," by Frank Palacio. ISBN 978-0-578-92612-4.

Published 2021 by Belizeobama Publisher Inc.

CONTENTS

INTRODUCTION

Watching the news daily, for countless hours over the past couple of years in particular, I observed that the words they use are often interesting, new, and varied. The news has a vocabulary of its own.

The topics on the news -- whether local, national, or international, are a driving force that created this new language. Every channel I tuned into seemed to be using these same words and terms, such as: *canary in the coal mine, cancel culture, conflate, contextualize, deflect, deep state conspiracy theory, pivot, political calculus, messaging, racial reckoning, structural racism, weaponize, white privilege, woke,* and so on.

I had to figure them out and learn them like a new language. Some were easy but others needed much more effort. Being a fairly intelligent person, as well as a teacher, I used my college background in: English, economics, political science, plus two years of law school. Combined with my love for learning, I listened actively to the news, taking notes, and consulting Google regularly whenever I have doubts or need information. I am now able to understand the evening news. Hence, I came up with the idea for this book and named it "An MSNBC, Fox News, And CNN Education: Words and Terms for the Educated and Uneducated used by Cooper, Cuomo, D. Lemon, and More." I decided to compile a list that would help any listener, who seeks self-improvement and who wants to learn to use these words, terms, and sayings in context.

A "News" Junkie.

Do you love MSNBC, Fox News, or CNN? Are you a "news" junkie? Do you suffer from twitching, itching, or break out in hives if you can't watch the evening news for once in your life? Maybe your TV wasn't working or you had another commitment. Friends came over and forced you to watch something else, so you missed the news and you felt out of sorts-- not your usual self. Have you ever gone an entire day without deodorant? Uncomfortable right? Going without news is almost as bad as going without deodorant, right?

My definition of a news junkie would be someone who is obsessed with watching news and must watch it as faithfully or as religiously or as compulsively as one who has to: exercise, diet, or check social media and so on.

My father, who was my biggest role model, was also faithful about watching the news. He worked hard often two jobs to support his family of seven. Watching the news, from a kid's, perspective was one of his biggest joys in life. He was a big looming figure with a kindly face and a ready laugh. But he could also be a disciplinarian and did not tolerate dissent.

"Turn off the music please. Let's turn to the news." We heard this often.

I tried to protest, "But we listened to the news yesterday, dad!"

"That was yesterday, my boy," dad said smiling. "News happens every day and I want to be informed and you should be informed, too!" I had never won an argument with my dad. Our score card was Dad 100 me 0.

Fareed Zakaria: One of the best minds on the planet
(1 of 25 guests and hosts from MSNBC, Fox News, and CNN, etc. featured in this book).

Fareed is an expert on International relations/politics with lots of books and research under his belt. Clearly, he is a brilliant mind and a deep thinker. Because of his non- European, although, good looks and charming accent, you might dismiss him casually out of prejudice or bias. Maybe you are an "America First" type of person and don't think that someone with an accent can tell you anything. Maybe you are a trump supporter who feels threatened by minorities or who looks down at minorities, so check yourself—I hope you have a sense of humor.

"How did a multi-millionaire fool everyday Americans into believing he was 'just an ordinary guy' just like them and win the presidency?"

Fareed wanted to know. So, he did valuable research and shared his findings on national television. Hillary Clinton and the entire field of candidates tried to tell us. "Trump is a con-man. He is a scam artist. He is a phony and a fraud. He is morally bankrupt. He has filed bankruptcy many times." They kept hammering away at candidate Trump. Why didn't America listen?

Criminals in California are allowed three strikes before they are locked away for life. Trump seemed to have a litany of sins and shady dealings that would have prevented him from being elected dog catcher in an old TV Western town movie. So why did he rise to the top of the heap? He won the coveted spot, the presidency of the most powerful country on earth. Why? A perplexed Zakaria, with blazing eyes like an evangelical preacher, wanted to know. A stunned, bruised and battered Hillary Clinton probably wanted to know. Barbers in their barbershops gnashed their teeth in fury. Most black barbers, at least, probably did. Hillary Clinton was described as the most qualified person ever to run for that office.

Feminists wanted to know. Trump had been caught on a hot mic saying that he had no problems grabbing women by the private part. The feminists were not happy with Trump's victory. Trump did not know how he had won. What a shocker what a stunner. Trump is known as a B.S. artist.

In his heart of heart, he knows this himself. He relishes telling jokes, tales, lies and outright whoppers. This is fun for him. He mocks people using outlandish facial expressions not seen since most people were in third grade and he mimics voices and expressions better than a first-rate paid comedian. Fareed made an entire show and production to describe and explain one of the most incredible con jobs or heists in history—how a con-man fooled ordinary everyday Americans into believing he was one of them and won the presidency.

Part I:
Words and Terms:

1. **Amnesia** refers to the loss of memories, such as facts, information and experiences. Though forgetting your identity is a common plot device in movies and television, that's not generally the case in real-life amnesia. Instead, people with amnesia — also called amnestic syndrome — usually know who they are.

   Example: Most politicians have a case of amnesia when it comes to keeping all their campaign promises.

2. **anarchy** Anarchism is a political philosophy and movement that is skeptical of authority and rejects all involuntary, coercive forms of hierarchy.

   Example: Some anarchists call for the abolition of the state, which they hold to be undesirable, unnecessary, and harmful.

3. **Antifa** short for antifascism; a political protest movement comprising autonomous groups affiliated by their militant opposition to fascism and other forms of extreme right-wing ideology.

   Example: Many protests were held by Antifa in connection with the death of George Floyd, an unarmed black man.

4. **antithesis** directly opposed or contrasted; mutually incompatible.

   Example: A selfish egomaniacal president is the antithesis of what President Obama stood for.

5. **articulate** to express an idea or feeling fluently and coherently. Referring to words having or showing the ability to speak fluently
   and coherently.

Example: The president was able to articulate his ideas of anti-immigrant sentiments to his "Birther Movement" and Proud Boys followers.

6. **aspirational** associated with or suggestive of a high level of success and social status and therefore appealing to people who <u>aspire</u> to such status
Example: A desire to have one hundred percent of the population vaccinated for Covid 19 is more aspirational than realistic.

7. **asymptomatic** of a condition or a person producing or showing no symptoms.

   Example: Many people have tested asymptomatic for Covid-19.

8. **asynchronous** of two or more objects or events, not existing or happening at the same time.

   Example: Asynchronous instruction for students is a time of independent study, where they can work on any subject they choose.

9. **base (the base)** consisting of dissimilar or diverse ingredients or constituents: mixed an ethnically heterogeneous population.

   Example: The base of the President's supporters are mainly Evangelical Christians and members of the radical right.

10. **benchmark** something that serves as a standard by which others may be measured or judged a stock whose performance is a benchmark against which other stocks can be measured.

    Example: By most benchmarks or criteria, Barack Obama had a successful presidency.

11. **bipartisan** involving the agreement or cooperation of two political parties that usually oppose each other's policies.

Example: The plan to defund the police was not a bipartisan one.

12. **BOLO** Be on the lookout.

Example: You have been warned BOLO!

13. **brinkmanship** the art or practice of pursuing a dangerous policy to the limits of safety before stopping, especially in politics.

Example: North Korea and the United States have been engaged in a game of brinkmanship to see who will come to the negotiating table first.

14. **capitalism** an economic and political system in which a country's trade and industry are controlled by private owners for profit, rather than by the state.

Example: Under capitalism, there are more billionaires than in countries where there is socialism.

15. **caveat** a warning or proviso of specific stipulations, conditions, or limitations.

Example: Since it was the young girl's first time getting pulled over, the police officer let her off with the caveat that next time he would not be so lenient.

16. **chicanery** the use of trickery to achieve a political, financial, or legal purpose.

Example: The leader resorted to chicanery in an attempt to overturn the results of the elections after he lost.

17. **comorbidities** the simultaneous presence of two or more diseases or medical conditions in a patient.

    Example: The patient had a difficult recovery from a minor cold due to underlying pre-conditions and comorbidities.

18. **concede** admit that something is true or valid after first denying or resisting it.

    Example: The former president did not want to concede that Joe Biden won the elections.

19. **conflate** combine (two or more texts, ideas, etc.) into one.

    Example: The issue of race and standardized tests are often conflated unless they are disaggregated.

20. **covid** an acute respiratory illness in humans caused by a coronavirus, capable of producing severe symptoms and in some cases death, especially in older people and those with underlying health conditions. It was originally identified in China in 2019 and became pandemic in 2020.

    Example: The Covid-19 is a disease that became a worldwide pandemic.

21. **co-opt** to choose or elect as a member; members co-opted to the committee. to appoint as a colleague or assistant. to take into a group (such as a faction, movement, or culture): absorb, assimilate.

    Example: *The students are co-opted by a system they serve even in their struggle against it.*

22. **cringeworthy** so embarrassing, awkward, or upsetting as to cause one to cringe.

Example: The amount of lies told by the former president is very cringeworthy.

23. **deflect** cause (something) to change direction by interposing something; turn aside from a straight course.

   Example: Politicians often like to deflect when asked tough questions.

24. **democrat** a member of the democratic party. The modern Democratic Party emphasizes social equality and equal opportunity. Democrats support voting rights and minority rights, including LGBT rights. The party championed the Civil Rights Act of 1964, which for the first time outlawed segregation.

   Example: A democrat usually supports more social programs than a republican.

25. **dialogue** conversation between two or more people as a feature of a book, play, or movie.

   Example: More dialogue is needed between parents and their children; so that better understanding and trust can be established for healthy relationships.

26. **disenfranchise** deprive (someone) of the right to vote.

   Example: Laws that require extra identification may cause many voters to become disenfranchised.

27. **disinformation** false information deliberately and often covertly spread (as by the planting of rumors) in order to influence public opinion or obscure the truth.

   Example: Most ruthless dictators use disinformation to maintain power.

28. disingenuous lacking in frankness, candor, or sincerity; falsely or hypocritically ingenuous; insincere.

Example: Her excuse for not voting while urging others to vote was rather disingenuous.

29. entitled believing oneself to be inherently deserving of privileges or special treatment.

Example: Some kids have forgotten the struggles of their parents and feel entitled as if the world owes them something.

30. faction a small, organized dissenting group within a larger one, especially in politics.

Example: Within the democratic party is a faction that believes in socialism.

31. fealty the obligation or the engagement to be faithful to a lord, usually sworn to by a vassal. fidelity; faithfulness. SYNONYMS FOR fealty.

Example: The movie star requested a pledge of loyalty or fealty from his employees, so he made them sign contracts not to write a tell all book.

32. fixer a person who makes arrangements for other people, especially of an illicit or devious kind.

Example: Michael Cohen testified that he was a fixer for Donald Trump.

33. gaslight manipulate (someone) by psychological means into questioning their own sanity.

Example: Some politicians like to gaslight those who are not well informed or educated.

34. generational means relating to a particular generation, or to the relationship between particular generation

35. gravitas dignity, seriousness, or solemnity of manner.

Example: Senators are expected to conduct themselves with a certain amount of gravitas.

36. gridlock a traffic jam affecting a whole network of intersecting streets. Also known as deadlock.

Example: There is inaction or gridlock in congress because both parties refuse to compromise.

37. grifter a con artist: someone who swindles people out of money through fraud. Grifters are also known as chiselers, defrauders, gougers, scammers, swindlers, and flim-flam men.

Example: The man refused steady employment and lived as a homeless grifter.

38. handler responsible for making sure that the talent knows when they are to perform, where they are to perform, and what time ...

39. hegemony the dominance of one group over another, often supported by legitimating norms and ideas. The associated term hegemon is used to identify the actor, group, class, or state that exercises hegemonic power or that is responsible for the dissemination of hegemonic ideas.

Example: The hegemony of the United States when it comes to popular culture is undeniable.

40. heterogeneous consisting of dissimilar or diverse ingredients or constituents: mixed an ethnically heterogeneous population.

Example: People of the same race can still be heterogeneous in terms of height, weight, eye color etc.

41. homogeneous of the same or a similar kind or nature. 2: of uniform structure or composition throughout. Examples: Stir in the flour, water, eggs, and sugar until it all blends together into one homogeneous mixture.

Example: Japan is often considered as a country with a homogeneous population when it comes to race and ethnicity.

42. hyperbole exaggerated statements or claims not meant to be taken literally.

Example: If you say you are as hungry as a bear then you would probably be using hyperbole.

43. impeachment a charge of misconduct made against the holder of a public office.

Example: The President's lawless and reckless conduct led to his impeachment.

44. infrastructure the basic physical and organizational structures and facilities (e.g., buildings, roads, power supplies) needed for the operation of a society or enterprise.

Example: The new government needs to focus building the nation's roads, highways, bridges, in other words infrastructure.

45. **influencer** a person with the ability to influence potential buyers of a product or service by promoting or recommending the items on social media. "Influencers can add serious credibility to your brand."

45. **innuendo** an allusive or oblique remark or hint, typically a suggestive or disparaging one.

   Example: Gossip and innuendo were the basis of the man's testimony.

46. **intel** useful information concerning a subject of interest such as an enemy.

   Example: Reliable intel was used before the bombs were unleashed.

47. **jingoism** extreme patriotism, especially in the form of aggressive or warlike foreign policy.

   Example: Many of the attacks on Asians after the Covid-19 pandemic is due to American jingoism.

48. **leverage** to hold the advantage in a situation or the stronger position in a contest, physical or otherwise. The lever is a tool for getting more work done with less physical force. With the right leverage, you might be able to lift a heavy box.

49. **liberal** willing to respect or accept behavior or opinions different from one's own; open to new ideas. (in a political context) favoring policies that are socially progressive and promote social welfare.

   Example: People's attitudes towards abortion is more liberal in some States than others.

50. **Machiavellian** cunning, scheming, and unscrupulous, especially in politics. "A whole range of outrageous Machiavellian maneuvers"

     Example: A skillful politician sometimes has to balance the needs of his community versus what is right in order to not act in a Machiavellian way.

51. **marginalized** (of a person, group, or concept) treated as insignificant or peripheral.

     Example: Marginalized cultural groups often band together to network and gain power.

52. **megalomaniac** a pathological egotist, that is, someone with a psychological disorder with symptoms like delusions of grandeur and an obsession with power. We also use the word megalomaniac more informally for people who behave as if they're convinced of their absolute power and greatness.

     Example: A megalomaniac often thinks that he is indispensable.

53. **messaging** a system or process of transmitting messages, especially electronically, by computer, telephone, television cable, etc.

     Example: His messaging system to his base of 75 million followers is done mostly through his use of twitter.

54. **mandate** an official order or commission to do something.

     Example: Joe Biden has received a mandate from the socialist elements of his party to hire more minorities to work for in his administration.

55. manifesto a public declaration of policy and aims, especially one issued before an election by a political party or candidate.

Example: In his manifesto the politician stated that he would ban certain pollutants and pesticides.

56. milieu the physical or social setting in which something occurs or develops.

Example: The study of Beethoven would include the milieu that influenced his work.

57. misinformation false or inaccurate information that is communicated regardless of an intention to deceive. Examples of misinformation are false rumors, insults, and pranks.

Example: In a court of law, the judge is usually careful to separate facts from misinformation.

58. monolithic of an organization or system) large, powerful, and intractably indivisible and uniform.

Example: The voters spoke through Brexit, rejecting any move toward a monolithic European superstate.

59. nationalism identification with one's own nation and support for its interests, especially to the exclusion or detriment of the interests of other nations.

Example: Nationalism, to be proud of one's heritage has its place.

60. nativism the policy of protecting the interests of native-born or established inhabitants against those of immigrants.

Example: Nativism can be described as a return to or emphasis on traditional or local customs, in opposition to outside influences.

61. narrative a spoken or written account of connected events; a story.

Example: The narrative that most members of the LGBTQ community are deviants was one that was promoted by some scientists in the 1960s.

62. Neo-Nazism Neo-Nazism refers to the post-World War II militant,.social, and political movements seeking to revive and implement Nazi ideology.

Example: Neo-Nazis often seek to employ people who think like they do.

63. normalize to make conform to or reduce to a norm or standard normalize blood pressure. Other Words from normalize include normalization.

Example: Some behaviors have become almost normalized in society today such as the pervasive use cellphone in public.

64. nuance a subtle difference in or shade of meaning, expression, or sound.

Example: The politician gave a nuanced answer in order to avoid telling a lie.

65. optics (typically in a political context) the way in which an event or course of action is perceived by the public.

Example: the optics of a doctor taking money from lobbyists for tobacco and alcohol companies seem immoral.

66. PAC in the United States, a political action committee (PAC) is a 527 organization that pools campaign contributions from members and donates those funds to campaigns for or against candidates, ballot initiatives, or legislation. The legal term PAC has been created in pursuit of campaign finance reform in the United States. This term is quite specific to all activities of campaign finance in the United States.

67. panacea a solution or remedy for all difficulties or diseases.

Example: Increasing welfare benefits, without asking people to be responsible for their own health and sobriety, seems more like a panacea than a cure for poverty.

68. pander gratify or indulge (an immoral or distasteful desire, need, or habit or a person with such a desire, etc.).

Example: The liquor store that panders to drug dealers and prostitutes enables them by selling drug paraphernalia that encourage addiction.

69. persona a persona is the image or personality that a person presents in public or in a specific setting—as opposed to their true self. The word is especially used in the phrase public persona, referring to the personality that a person presents in public and that they are known for by most people.

70. pivot a movement in which the player holding the ball may move in any direction with one foot, while keeping the other (the pivot foot) in contact with the floor.

Example: Politicians like to pivot to avoid responsibility.

71. platform the declared policy of a political party or group.

Example: Republican politicians often seek election on a platform of low taxes.

72. posturing behavior that is intended to impress or mislead.

Example: Political posturing made the Senator who hates guns to appear in a pro-gun advertisement.

73. pundit an expert in a particular subject or field who is frequently called on to give opinions about it to the public.

Example: The pundit predicted that Obama would win a 2nd term in office.

74. pro-gun favoring the right to own guns and opposing legislation restricting this right.

Example: The pro-gun activists held their meeting at a shooting range.

75. pro-life opposed to abortion.

Example: Most Christians are a hundred percent pro-life.

76. poll a questioning or canvassing of persons selected at random or by quota to obtain information or opinions to be analyzed and a record of the information so obtained.

Example: A real leader does not always govern by what is popular; but rather by what is the right thing to do.

77. quagmire soft miry land that shakes or yields under the foot. a difficult, precarious, or entrapping position or predicament.

Example: The quagmire that is known as the Iraq War lasted longer than any other war in the past 100 years.

78. quarantine a term during which a ship arriving in port and suspected of carrying contagious disease is held in isolation from the shore.

Example: In the movie, the scientists that came in contact with leprosy had to be put in quarantine to make sure they weren't contaminated.

79. racism prejudice, discrimination, or antagonism directed against a person or people on the basis of their membership in a particular racial or ethnic group, typically one that is a minority or marginalized.

Example: Racism is a problem in many countries with heterogeneous populations.

80. radicalize cause (someone) to adopt radical positions on political or social issues.

Example: Some of those involved in the peace protest had been radicalized by the Vietnam War.

81. reckoning the action or process of calculating or estimating something or a bill or account, or its settlement.

Example: Last year was not, by any reckoning, a particularly good one.

82. reparation the making of amends for a wrong one has done, by paying money to or otherwise helping those who have been wronged

Example: Some African Americans believe that they deserve reparation for the enslavement of their ancestors.

83. the right traditional attitudes and practices and conservative policies

Example: Voters who are on the right are usually anti-abortion.

84. regime a government, especially an authoritarian one

Example: Some regimes in Asia employ death squads to suppress calls for democracy.

85. rhetoric the art of effective or persuasive speaking or writing, especially the use of figures of speech and other compositional techniques

Example: The politicians on both sides of the issue need to tone down the inflammatory language and tone down the rhetoric.

86. shenanigans secret or dishonest activity or maneuvering. silly or high-spirited behavior; mischief

Example: Widespread financial shenanigans had ruined the fortunes of many during the stock market crash.

87. sketchy use to describe someone who creates an impression of unsavoriness, or something that comes from an untrustworthy source or is itself untrustworthy

Example: The salesman was described as a sketchy person with a history of allegations of financial allegations filed against him.

88. socialism a political and economic theory of social organization which advocates that the means of production, distribution, and exchange should be owned or regulated by the community as a whole

Example: Many countries in Europe are governed by some type of socialism.

89. sociopath a person with a personality disorder manifesting itself in extreme antisocial attitudes and behavior and a lack of conscience

Example: Most serial killers are described as being cold hearted sociopaths.

90. spin to give a news story or other information a particular interpretation, especially a favorable one

Example: After the elections, the spin was that Trump lost because the elections were rigged.

91. spinmeister a media liaison or spokesperson, charged with presenting the spin for their political side

Example: The lobbyist is basically a spinmeister for the cigarette industry.

92. status quo the existing state of affairs, especially regarding social or political issues

Example: Often times the police have a vested interest in maintaining the status quo.

93. stimulus a thing or event that evokes a specific functional reaction in an organ or tissue

Example: The stimulus that caused the fight was when one boy mentioned the other's "mama".

94. stymie prevent or hinder the progress of

Example: Things that can stymie creativity include excessive drug and alcohol use.

95. tactician a person who uses a carefully planned strategy to achieve a specific end

Example: Most military generals aspire to be brilliant tacticians in battle.

96. template a shaped piece of metal, wood, card, plastic, or other material used as a pattern for processes such as painting, cutting out, shaping, or drilling

Example: The engineer was expected to follow the exact specifications of the template.

97. toxic referring to a person, is anyone whose behavior adds negativity and upset to your life

Example: Many times, people who are toxic are dealing with their own stresses and traumas.

98. transactional relating to the conducting of business, especially buying or selling
Example: The relationship between the doctor and the patient was strictly transactional. The doctor provided the services and the patient paid for them in full.

99. transparency as used in science, engineering, business, the humanities and in other social contexts, is operating in such a way that it is easy for others to see what actions are performed. Transparency implies openness, communication, and accountability.

Example: The new president promised transparency in dealing with the press unlike the prior administration.

100. tribalism the behavior and attitudes that stem from strong loyalty to one's own tribe or social group

Example: Cultural tribalism is evident and dangerous when people vote for the person rather than the policy or idea.

101. trope a figurative or metaphorical use of a word or expression a significant or recurrent theme; a motif.

Example: The demonization of blacks as lazy and not as intelligent is a trope that has been around for centuries.

102. Trumpism a term for the political ideology, style of governance, political movement and set of mechanisms for acquiring and keeping power that are associated with the 45th president of the United States, Donald Trump, and his political base.

Example: Trumpism is becoming synonymous with the views of the new Republican party

103. wackadoodle an eccentric or fanatical person

Example: Many wackadoodles who belong to the cult predict the world will end in a year or two.

104. weaponize adapt for use as a weapon

Example: The illicit laboratory produced and weaponized many deadly biological agents, including anthrax.

105. wheelhouse one's area of interest or expertise

Example: the high-powered lawyer said that gourmet cooking was not in his wheelhouse.

106. whistle-blower a person who informs on a person or organization engaged in an illicit activity

Example: A closed door hearing was held to protect the whistle-blower's identity.

107. woke Through the 2000s and early 2010s, *woke* was used either as a term for not literally falling asleep, or as slang for one's suspicions of being cheated on by a romantic partner. In the 21st-century's first decade, use of *woke* encompassed the earlier meaning with an added sense of being "alert to social and/or <u>racial discrimination</u> and injustice". This usage was popularized by soul singer <u>Erykah Badu</u>'s 2008 song "<u>Master Teacher</u>", via the song's refrain, "I stay woke". https://en.wikipedia.org/wiki/Woke

108. xenophobia dislike of or prejudice against people from other countries

Example: The resurgence of racism and xenophobia are one of the many problems facing our country at the moment.

109. Zoom the leader in modern enterprise video communications, with an easy, reliable cloud platform for video and audio conferencing, chat, and webinars.

Example: The business meeting and the office party were both held via Zoom.

Terms and Expressions:

1. **alternative facts** a phrase used by U.S. Counselor to the President Kellyanne Conway during a Meet the Press interview on January 22, 2017, in which she defended White House Press Secretary Sean Spicer's false statement about the attendance numbers of Donald Trump's inauguration as President of the United States.

    Example: The use of the term "alternative facts" was designed to lie and obfuscate.

2. **Achilles heel** a weakness in spite of overall strength, which can lead to downfall. While the mythological origin refers to a physical vulnerability, idiomatic references to other attributes or qualities that can lead to downfall are common.

    Example: The only weakness in Shaquille's game was his inability to shoot free throws, which was his Achilles heel.

3. **alternate universe** also known as a parallel universe, or alternate reality, is a hypothetical self-contained plane of existence, co-existing with one's own. The sum of all potential parallel universes that constitute reality is often called a "multiverse".

4. **America's Original Sin** Racism is America's original sin according to Jim Wallis, an author, activist, preacher, teacher, and pastor. The book calls for Americans to overcome racism in the United States, issuing an appeal rooted in fundamental Christian values. It argues in favor of telling the truth about the American past, suggesting that this is essential to national redemption. The book also discusses the concept of white privilege, arguing that it constitutes a sin.

   Example: America needs to come to terms with its past and the fight for social justice can be traced back to "America's original sin".

5. **analysis paralysis** describes an individual or group process when overanalyzing or overthinking a situation can cause forward motion or decision-making to become "paralyzed", meaning that no solution or course of action is decided upon.

   Example: My mom used to always say not to flog a dead horse to death which often what analysis paralysis does.

6. **Black Lives Matter** is a movement that came to prominence in 2020. The group was very instrumental in changing the world following the police killing of an unarmed black man, George Floyd. The world watched in horror as Mr. Floyd died begging for oxygen to breathe and then begging for his mother as his captor extinguished the life out of him as the cameras rolled capturing it all for television for the world to view. The young founders of Black Lives Matter, Alicia Garcia, Patrisse Cullors, and Opal Tometi, took matters into their own hands because if they didn't no one else seemed able to. They generated protest, action, and protestors who took to the streets in huge numbers all over the world demanding justice for Floyd and all who had suffered in the past, present, and future from police brutality and structural racism.

7. **binary opposites** the system of language and/or thought by which two theoretical opposites are strictly defined and set off against one another. It is the contrast between two mutually exclusive terms, such as on and off, up and down, left and right. Binary opposition originated in Saussurean structuralist theory.

   *Example:*The senators were binary opposites in their attitude towards abortion.

8. **birther movement** Donald Trump was the most prominent promoter of the 'Birther Movement' against Barack Obama, repeatedly questioning if he was foreign-born, and infamously demanding his birth certificate. 'Birtherism' is a movement and essentially a conspiracy theory which claims that former US President Barack Obama was born abroad and was, as a result, ineligible to be the president. Similarly, a 'birther' is a person who subscribes to or promotes this incorrect belief.

9. **blind loyalty** involves being loyal to a person or cause despite the damage the person or cause does to himself or herself or others. Excusing bad behavior in the name of protecting allegiance to another seems honorable at first, but is ultimately dangerous as silence is a form of collusion.

   Example: Unless you are willing to exhibit blind loyalty to the Senator, he refuses to hire you.

10. **body politic** the people of a nation, state, or society considered collectively as an organized group of citizens.

    Example: The democratic party is a big tent with many ideas that are woven into their body politic.

11. **boots on the ground** a relatively new military idiom that is slowly making its way into general use. Boots on the

ground refers to active ground troops in a military campaign, men or women who are physically present and fighting in a war zone.

Example: Most wars in the future are not going to be fought with boots on the ground, but by drone.

12. **bread and butter issue** is one that affects everyday people, like tax rates or road conditions. Basic, fundamental matters are bread-and-butter issues. Issues that have some connection to money are often described this way too, especially by politicians and journalists.

Example: Voters are more concerned about bread and butter issues that affect their pocketbook like taxes.

13. **buzz words** a word or phrase, new or already existing, that becomes very popular for a period of time. Buzz words often derive from technical terms yet often have much of the original technical meaning removed through fashionable use, being simply used to impress others.

Example: Teachers like to include certain buzz words when testing specific topics.

14. **cabin fever** describes the psychological symptoms that a person may experience when they are confined to their home for extended periods. Such symptoms may include feelings of restlessness, irritability, and loneliness.

Example: After being cooped up during the pandemic most parents and their children were experiencing cabin fever and wanted to enjoy outdoor activities.

15. **canary in a coal mine** an allusion to caged canaries (birds) that miners would carry down into the mine tunnels with them. If dangerous gases such as carbon monoxide collected in the mine, the gases would kill the canary before

killing the miners, thus providing a warning to exit the tunnels immediately. Something whose sensitivity to adverse conditions makes it a useful early indicator of such conditions; something which warns of the coming of greater danger or trouble by a deterioration in its health or welfare.

16. **cancel culture** "to dismiss something or somebody" and "to reject an individual or idea." And when people use the term unironically, it reveals a big problem with our culture. ... Cancel culture as it currently exists doesn't give people a chance to learn from or apologize for their wrongdoings.

17. **cause for pause** to cause (someone) to stop and think about something carefully or to have doubts about something.

    Example: I was going to ask her for help, but the look on her face gave me pause.

18. **cautionary tale** a tale told in folklore, to warn its listener of a danger. There are three essential parts to a cautionary tale, though they can be introduced in a large variety of ways. First, a taboo or prohibition is stated: some act, location, or thing is said to be dangerous.

    Example: His life is a like a cautionary tale because nobody should tell 3,000 lies and not get impeached.

19. **coattail effect** the down-ballot or coattail effect is the tendency for a popular political party leader to attract votes for other candidates of the same party in an election. A popular statewide candidate for governor or senator can attract support for down ballot races of their party as well.

    Example: The leader of the party was so popular, that all the other members of his party were able to win their election races as well due to the coattail effect.

20. contact tracing contact tracing is when public health workers identify and notify the people who were exposed to infected people. They let them know that they've been in close contact with an infected person, and what to do next to keep themselves and their loved ones safe. Public health departments have used contact tracing for decades to fight the spread of infectious diseases.

Example: Contact tracing is important to stem the tide of the virus, so that people can be warned of others that are infected.

21. coup d'état the removal and seizure of a government and its powers. Typically, it is an illegal, unconstitutional seizure of power by a political faction.

Example: Some people believe that the resurrection on January 6th was an attempted coup d'état.

22. covid fatigue It's real and it's strong. Both the intensity and the length of time of COVID-19 stress takes a toll on everyone. We're tired of being
cooped up, tired of being careful, tired of being scared. Many people understand this, which adds to their exhaustion and stress.

Example: Children can also suffer from covid fatigue and they long to go back to the way things were before.

23. crossing the Rubicon refers to any individual or group committing itself irrevocably to a risky or revolutionary course of action, similar to the modern phrase "passing the point of no return".

Example: Once the leader said they were marching to the Capitol to "stop the steal" there was no turning back; they had crossed the Rubicon.

24. crowd sourcing obtain (information or input into a particular task or project) by enlisting the services of a large number of people, either paid or unpaid, typically via the internet.

Example: She crowdsourced advice on the best gifts for valentine on Google.

25. cult of personality a cult of personality, or cult of the leader, arises when a country's regime or, more rarely, an individual uses the techniques of mass media, propaganda, the big lie, spectacle, the arts, patriotism, and government-organized demonstrations and rallies to create an idealized, heroic, and worshipful image of a an individual.

Example: Some politicians are very charismatic and can be described as cult of personality.

26. culture war a cultural conflict between social groups and the struggle for dominance of their values, beliefs, and practices. It commonly refers to topics on which there is general societal disagreement and polarization in societal values is seen.

Example: In a multiracial multiethnic society there are culture wars about social justice issues such as busing and the appropriateness of cultural attire in certain milieus.

27. currency of hate although it's not officially designated as one, hate has become a dominant currency over the past 25 years or so. For millions, hate is as much a currency today as the money (or lack of) in their wallets. *A.G. Dumas, Hate As Currency, Wilderness House Literary Review 14/3*

28. deep pockets is an American slang term; it usually means "extensive financial wealth or resources". It is usually used in reference to big companies or organizations (ex: the

American tobacco companies have "deep pockets"), although it can be used in reference to wealthy individuals (e.g., Bill Gates, Warren Buffett).

Example: Lawyers usually go after the people with deep pockets when filing lawsuits.

29. **deep state conspiracy theory** a theory which suggests that collusion and cronyism exist within the U.S. political system and constitute a hidden government within the legitimately elected government. Author Mike Lofgren believes that there is "a hybrid association of elements of government and parts of top-level finance and industry that is effectively able to govern the United States without reference to the consent of the governed as expressed through the formal political process," or consider the deep state to encompass corruption prevalent among career politicians and civil servants. The 'deep state' theory has been dismissed by authors for *The New York Times* and *The New York Observer*. University of Miami Professor Joseph Uscinski says, "The concept has always been very popular among conspiracy theorists, whether they call it a deep state or something else."

30. **digital footprints** the information about a particular person that exists on the internet as a result of their online activity.

Example: The computer teacher taught the students that their digital footprint can do damage to their reputation.

31. **dog-whistle** a high-pitched whistle used to train dogs, typically having a sound inaudible to humans. A subtly aimed political message which is intended for, and can only be understood by, a particular group.

Example: Talking in code and nuanced language is often a dog-whistle to people of similar beliefs.

32. domestic terrorism the unlawful use, or threatened use, of violence by a group or individual based and operating entirely within the United States (or its territories) without foreign direction committed against persons or property to intimidate or coerce a government, the civilian population, or any segment thereof, in furtherance of political or social objectives.

FBI — The Terrorist Threat Confronting the United Stateswww.fbi.gov › news › testimony › the-terrorist-threat-c...

33. double down strengthen one's commitment to a particular strategy or course of action, typically one that is potentially risky.

Example: trump never apologizes or admits to making mistakes; he prefers to double down.

34. echo chamber an environment where a person only encounters information or opinions that reflect and reinforce their own.

Example: Political conventions are often an echo chamber for people with the same ideas and beliefs.

35. existential threat a threat to something's very existence— when the continued being of something is at stake or in danger. It is used to describe threats to actual living things as well to nonliving thing things, such as a country or an ideology.

Example: A leader that is so divisive, incompetent, and doesn't follow "the science" can be described as an existential threat.

36. fact check investigate (an issue) in order to verify the facts.

Example: We didn't fact-check the assertions in the opinion article in the newspaper.

37. fake news is false or misleading information presented as news. It often has the aim of damaging the reputation of a person or entity, or making money through revenue. Media scholar Nolan Higdon has offered a broader definition of fake news as "false or misleading content presented as news and communicated in formats spanning spoken, written, printed, electronic, and digital communication."

Example: Whenever a politician is caught with their hand in the cookie jar, they say, "I'm innocent that's just fake news."

38. false equivalent a logical fallacy in which an equivalence is drawn between two subjects based on flawed or false reasoning. This fallacy is categorized as a fallacy of inconsistency. Colloquially, a false equivalence is often called "comparing apples and oranges."

Example: To compare the Black Lives Matter organization to the Ku Klux Klan is an Example:of a false equivalency.

39. false narrative a subtler and more dangerous form of misinformation. The Example:of immigrants also illustrates this problem. Several fake news stories share the underlying narrative that thousands of criminals and terrorists are supposedly pouring across our borders.

Example: To blame the group Antifa, and not the Trump supporters, as being responsible for the DC riot is a false narrative.

40. force of nature When you call someone a force of nature it means the person has a strong personality or character like a hurricane or a tsunami, they might be full of energy, unstoppable, unchallengeable, unforgettable. In summary, a person to be reckoned with.

Example: Kobe Bryant was a force of nature and a talent who broke many records in his basketball career.

41. free market an economic system in which prices are determined by unrestricted competition between privately owned businesses.

Example: Bartering sites where people can bid on electronic devices are an Example:of the free market at work.

42. frontline worker these are the people communities depend on in emergencies, such as firefighters and police.

Example: The frontline workers are given discounts at some restaurants as a show of appreciation for their many sacrifices during the pandemic

43. gunboat diplomacy foreign policy that is supported by the use or threat of military force.

Example: The US sent in Special Ops to rescue Americans from the embassy in Iraq which was an Example:of gunboat diplomacy.

44. herd immunity resistance to the spread of an infectious disease within a population that is based on pre-existing immunity of a high proportion of individuals as a result of previous infection or vaccination.

*Example:*Experts believe that the level of vaccination needed to achieve herd immunity varies by disease but ranges from 83 to 94 percent.

45. hijack an issue the act of taking control of or using something that does not belong to you for your own advantage, or an occasion when this happens.

Example: Racists have hijacked the issue of border security to blame jobless Mexican Americans for the high rate of unemployment.

46. hold feet to fire Also, keep someone's feet to the fire. Pressure someone to consent to or undertake something, as in the only way you'll get him to agree is to hold his feet to the fire. This idiom alludes to an ancient test of courage or form of torture in which a person's feet were so placed. It began to be used figuratively in the second half of the 1900s. Also see hold a gun to someone's head.

47. institutionalized racism institutional racism, also known as systemic racism, is a form of racism that is embedded as normal practice within society or an organization. It can lead to such issues as discrimination in criminal justice, employment, housing, health care, political power, and education, among other issues.

Example: The NAACP is a civil rights organization that is concerned with institutionalized racism in housing.

48. live in a bubble living in a bubble means to live in one's own world, completely isolated from what is happening all around. A person living in a bubble can't see or perceive events around him as he is too engrossed in the little world he has created for himself.

Example: Some people live in an alternate reality and are insulated from reality as if they live in a bubble.

49. long game having a long-term plan, long term goals, or doing things now that set you up for the future. There are articles about playing the long game in the arenas of sex, dating, creativity, business strategy, education, and financial planning.

Example: The long game for some Republicans is to win future elections by using voter suppression tactics in some States.

50. low bar to be a remarkably low standard.

Example: Leaders such as mayors and governors who don't believe in science are operating at a pathetic low bar.

51. low hanging fruit a commonly used metaphor for doing the simplest or easiest work first, or for a quick fix that produces ripe, delectable results. In sales, it means a target that is easy to achieve, a product or service that is easy to sell, or a prospective client who seems very likely to buy the product, especially compared with other, more reluctant prospects.

52. modus operandi a particular way or method of doing something, especially one that is characteristic or well-established.

Example: His stock in trade or modus operandi was to attack, bully and fire people by tweets.

53. moral compass used in reference to a person's ability to judge what is right and wrong and act accordingly.

Example: He is by no means the only senior politician who has mislaid his moral compass.

54. moral equivalency is a term used in political debate, usually to deny that a moral comparison can be made of two sides in a conflict, or in the actions or tactics of two sides. The term had some currency in polemic debates about the Cold War, and currently the Arab–Israeli conflict.

Example: There is no moral equivalency between the peaceful protests led by Black Lives Matter and the terror inflicted by the Ku Klux Klan.

55. **new normal** a new normal is a state to which an economy, society, etc. settles following a crisis, when this differs from the situation that prevailed prior to the start of the crisis.

Example: Wearing face masks has become a new normal as the result of the pandemic.

56. **a nothing burger** something that is or turns out to be insignificant or lacking in substance.

Example: A "another nothingburger of a debate" is what the conflict was described as being.

57. **one issue voter** Single-issue politics are a form of litmus test; common examples are abortion, taxation, animal rights, environment, and guns. The National Rifle Association in the United States, which has only one specific interest, is an example of a single-issue group. What differentiates single-issue groups from other interest groups is their intense style of lobbying.

Example: Some one-issue voters are willing to overlook President Trump's behavior on Twitter because they think he's good for the economy.

58. **one-trick pony** a person or thing with only one special feature, talent, or area of expertise.

Example: Because of his limited skills the basketball player was a specialist but also a one-trick pony.

59. opposition research the practice of collecting information on a political opponent or other adversary that can be used to discredit or otherwise weaken them.

The information can include biographical, legal, criminal, medical, educational, or financial history or activities, as well as prior media coverage, or the voting record of a politician.

Example: Opposition research can also entail using "trackers" to follow an individual and record their activities or political speeches.

60. parallel universe also known as an alternate universe, or alternate reality, is a hypothetical self-contained plane of existence, co-existing with one's own. The sum of all potential parallel universes that constitute reality is often called a "multiverse".

Example: In this political climate today, it seems that Democrats and Republicans are living in parallel universes; they're not able to agree on much.

61. perfect storm A perfect storm is an event in which a rare combination of circumstances drastically aggravates the event.

Example: High unemployment followed by a pandemic were a perfect storm that decimated the economy.

62. plausible deniability is the ability of people, typically senior officials in a formal or informal chain of command, to deny knowledge of or responsibility for any damnable actions committed by others in an organizational hierarchy because of a lack or absence of evidence that can confirm their participation, even if they were personally involved in or at least willfully ignorant of the actions. If illegal or otherwise-disreputable and unpopular activities become public, high-ranking officials may deny any awareness of such acts to insulate themselves and shift the blame onto the agents who carried out the acts, as they are confident that their doubters will be unable to prove otherwise. The lack of evidence to the contrary ostensibly makes the denial plausible (credible), but sometimes, it makes the denial only unactionable.

63. polar opposites the diametrically opposite point of a circle or sphere. It is mathematically known as an antipodal point, or antipode when referring to the Earth. It is also an idiom often used to describe people and ideas that are opposites.

Example: Men and women are usually polar opposites on the issue of cuddling.

64. political calculus refers to calculation or reasoning of a specifically political nature and means to make evaluations and decisions which are primarily based upon politically expedient considerations, rather than ad as opposed to all other considerations (i.e., reality, principle, oral, ethical).

Example: The political calculus that most Republicans made is: it is better to defend Donald Trump than to call him out because of his power and influence.

65. political correctness the avoidance, often considered as taken to extremes, of forms of expression or action that are perceived to exclude, marginalize, or insult groups of people who are socially disadvantaged or discriminated against.

Example: Some books have been banned because of political correctness.

66. **politically expedient** something you do to advance yourself politically. Use expedient when you want to hint that a particular solution or strategy has certain benefits and advantages but is not completely fair.

    Example: It may seem politically expedient for a mayor to attend church regularly only 6 months before elections are held.

67. **political suicide** political suicide is a concept by which a politician or political party loses widespread support and confidence from the voting public by proposing actions that are seen as unfavorable or that might threaten the status quo.

    Example: To espouse bigamy is probably political suicide for a President of the USA.

68. **Presidential Daily Briefs** is a daily summary of high-level, all-source information and analysis on national security issues produced for the president and key cabinet members and advisers.

69. **Proud Boys** a far-right, neo-fascist, and male-only white nationalist organization that promotes and engages in political violence in the United States and Canada. The group originated in the far-right Taki's Magazine in 2016 under the leadership of Vice Media co-founder and former commentator Gavin McInnes, taking its name from the song "Proud of Your Boy" from the 2011 Disney musical Aladdin.

    Example: many in that Proud Boys organization are big fans of Donald Trump.

70. **push back** disagree with or oppose an action or proposal.

Example: There was push back from the Republicans when legislation was proposed to raise the minimum wage to $15 an hour.

71. quid pro quo a favor or advantage granted or expected in return for something

Example: The financial to Ukraine was going to be a quid pro quo for helping the president get salacious information on his opponent.

72. radical right in liberal democracies, the political right opposes socialism and social democracy. Right-wing parties include conservatives, Christian democrats, classical liberals, and nationalists, as well as fascists on the far-right.

Example: Many members of the radical right are against the Antifa elements of the democratic party.

73. racial reckoning The killing of several unarmed blacks by police precipitated a national American cultural reckoning on topics of racial injustice. Public opinion of racism and discrimination quickly shifted in the wake of the protests, with significantly increased support of the Black Lives Matter movement and acknowledgement of institutional racism. Demonstrators revived a public campaign for the removal of Confederate monuments and memorials as well as other historic symbols such as statues of venerated American slaveholders and modern display of the Confederate battle flag. Public backlash widened to other institutional symbols, including place names, namesakes, brands and cultural practices. Anti-racist self-education became a trend throughout June 2020 in the United States. Black anti-racist writers found new audiences and places on bestseller lists. American consumers also sought out black-owned businesses to support. The effects of American activism extended internationally, as global protests destroyed their own local symbols of racial injustice. Multiple media began to refer to it as a national reckoning on racial issues in early June. https://en.wikipedia.org/wiki/2020%E2%80%932021_United_States_racial_unres

Example: Our country has yet to come to terms with the abuse and horrors that were caused by slavery, therefore racial reckoning would entail restitution to make amends.

74. remote learning occurs when the learner and instructor, or source of information, are separated by time and distance and therefore cannot meet in a traditional classroom setting. Also referred to as Distance Education, Virtual Instruction, or Remote Training.

Example: Remote learning was available to some students during the pandemic.

75. revisionist history the distortion of the historical record such that certain events appear to have occurred and/or impacted history in a way that is in drastic disagreement with the historical record and/or consensus, and usually meant to advance a socio-political view or agenda.

Example: Some consider it revisionist history to take down statues of Christopher Columbus because of his treatment of the natives.

76. shake down to blackmail someone for money; to extort someone. A noun or pronoun is often used between "shake" and "down."

Example: The president was accused of shaking down the Ukrainians by demanding information about his political opponent.

77. **social distancing** also called "physical distancing," means keeping a safe space between yourself and other people who are not from your household.

    Example: If we practice social distancing, we can slow the spread of Covid-19.

78. **social justice** the view that everyone deserves equal economic, political and social rights and opportunities. Social workers aim to open the doors of access and opportunity for everyone, particularly those in greatest need."

    Example: social justice is important for a more equitable society.

79. **sound bite** a short extract from a recorded interview, chosen for its pungency or appropriateness. a brief recorded statement (as by a public figure) broadcast especially on a television news program. also, a brief catchy comment or saying.

    Example: The sound bite that was played by the news gave a one-sided picture that was deemed prejudicial to the defendant in the lawsuit.

80. **speak truth to power** Stand up for what's right and tell people in charge what's what. That's the idea behind the phrase speak truth to power, an expression for courageously confronting an authority, calling out injustices on their watch, and demanding change.

    Example: When the little guy stands up to a crooked politician and does the right thing, that is speaking truth to power.

81. **Stockholm syndrome** a psychological response which occurs when hostages or abuse victims bond with their

captors or abusers. This psychological connection develops over the course of the days, weeks, months, or even years of captivity or abuse.

Example: The kidnapped victim eventually participated in the crimes of her kidnappers due to the Stockholm syndrome theory.

82. **super spreader event** an event in which an infectious disease is spread much more than usual, while an unusually contagious organism infected with a disease is known as a super spreader. In the context of a human-borne illness, a super spreader is an individual who is more likely to infect others, compared with a typical infected person.

Example: Such super spreader events are of particular concern in epidemiology.

83. **traffic in something** to deal in something; to trade in something, usually something illegal or traffic in lies, hates, or racism

Example: Some politicians traffic in lies by repeating the lie that Joe Biden stole the elections.

84. **talking point** a talking point in debate or discourse is a succinct statement designed to support persuasively one side taken on an issue. Such statements can either be free standing or created as retorts to the opposition's talking points and are frequently used in public relations, particularly in areas heavy in debate such as politics and marketing. A political think tank will strategize the most effective informational attack on a target topic and launch talking points from media personalities to saturate discourse in order to frame a debate in their favor, standardizing the responses of sympathizers to their unique cause.

Example: The politician had his spiel or talking points ready when asked about his views on abortion.

85. **systemic racism** refers to the oppressive racist realities that have been institutionalized and manifest in all of society's parts including the economy, politics, education, religion, family, etc. It includes (1) exploitative and discriminatory white practices targeting people of color, (2) institutionalized economic and other resource inequalities along racial lines, and (3) dominant racial frame generated to rationalize white privilege and dominance.

Example: Systemic racism occurs when blacks and minorities are discriminated against in housing or for home loans.

86. **Tea Party** a US political movement that emerged from a series of conservative protests against the federal government in 2009.

Example: The Tea Party, it was believed, was partly responsible for spreading the rumor that President Obama was not born in in the United States.

87. **the big lie** "The Big Lie." It's Democrats' shorthand for Trump's baseless and overwhelmingly debunked effort to call the results of the 2020 election into question — a set of claims that led his supporters to take drastic action in storming the U.S. Capitol. Aaron Blake, Feb. 12, 2021, Trump's 'Big Lie' was bigger than just a stolen election - Washington Post,

88. **there is no there** a descriptive phrase (originally coined by Gertrude Stein) now used to convey an utter lack of substance or veracity as it pertains to the subject under discussion.

Example: when it comes to whether our elections were rigged, there is no there because the elections were the safest we have probably ever had.

89. **tone down the rhetoric** to cause something to have less of an impact on the senses of sight or sound; to lessen the impact of something prepared for public performance or consumption.

Example: instead yelling at each other and name calling, both teams decided to tone down the rhetoric and let their play on the field do the talking.

90. **truth serum** a colloquial name for any of a range of psychoactive drugs used in an effort to obtain information from subjects who are unable or unwilling to provide it otherwise.

Example: Some politicians should be made to take a truth serum because they tell too many untruths.

91. **Uncle Tom** Although Stowe presents Uncle Tom as a virtuous man, the expression "Uncle Tom" is often used as a term of reproach for a subservient black person who tolerates discrimination.

Example: "Don't be an Uncle Tom; you should defend Black Lives Matter," my friend said.

92. **walk back** retract a statement or reverse an action or decision.

Example: "If you are given the chance to walk back your insensitive remarks you should do so."

93. **white privilege** the societal privilege that benefits white people over non-white people in some societies, particularly if they are otherwise under the same social,

political, or economic circumstances. With roots in European colonialism and imperialism, and the Atlantic slave trade, white privilege has developed in circumstances that have broadly sought to protect white racial privileges, various national citizenships and other rights or special benefits.

Example: Some whites have admitted that they have benefitted from white privilege, because they have never experienced structural racism.

94. **without a filter** the term 'without a filter' is a pretty common one used today to describe a person who speaks without tact, seems to blurt out their thoughts or is generally seen as very blunt. The phrase comes from the idea that your mouth says what your brain thinks without consideration to the audience, situation or time.

Example: Most comedians don't have a filter when they are performing on stage, and no topic is off limits.

95. **youth culture** the way children, adolescents, and young adults live, and the norms, values, and practices they share. Culture is the shared symbolic systems, and processes of maintaining and transforming those systems. Youth culture differs from the culture of older generations.

Example: Texting seems to be a staple of youth culture; whereas, someone from the 40s or 50s might not be as fond of texting.

96. **zero sum game** a situation in which one person or group can win something only by causing another person or group to lose it.

Example: We are all, Americans, therefore politics should not be viewed as a zero-sum game, but rather as a compromise for the benefit of all.

Part II:
Famous Proverbs, Quotes, and Sayings

1. **"Ask not what your country can do for you, ask what you can do for your country**

   Example: To inspire the country, the president quoted Kennedy saying, "Ask not what your country can do for you, ask what you can do for your country."

2. **crossing the Rubicon:** refers to any individual or group committing itself irrevocably to a risky or revolutionary course of action, similar to the modern phrase "passing the point of no return".

   Example: By cancelling diplomacy, the leader crossed the Rubicon and declared war immediately.

3. **Facts are stubborn thing:** "Facts are stubborn things; and whatever may be our wishes, our inclinations, or the dictates of our passion, they cannot alter the state of facts and evidence." https://www.goodreads.com/quotes/32621-facts-are-stubborn-things-and-whatever-may-be-our-wishes

   Example: When you deny science, you are denying certain facts and facts are stubborn things.

4. **gunboat diplomacy** In international politics, the term gunboat diplomacy refers to the pursuit of foreign policy objectives with the aid of conspicuous displays of naval power, implying or constituting a direct threat of warfare should terms not be agreeable to the superior force.

   Example: In a gunboat diplomacy move the Korean leader ceased peace talks and fired his missiles at will.

5. **Half a loaf is better than none** it is better to accept less than one wants or expects than to have nothing at all.

Example: When considering whether to take a low paying job or not, keep in mind that "Half a loaf is better than none."

6. **In the land of the blind the one-eyed man is king** Even someone with limited abilities or opportunities is dominant over, and considered special by, those who have even fewer abilities and ...

Example: We depended on my friend Juan to translate for us when we visited Spain because his limited Spanish was better than ours. We theorized that in the land of the blind the one-eyed man is king.

7. **Let the end justify the means** is used to say that a desired result is so good or important that any method, even a morally bad one, may be used to achieve it

Example: They believe that the **end justifies the means** and will do anything to get their candidate elected.

8. **Money is the mother's milk of politics** money is usually very important in order to run a political campaign and get your candidate elected.

Example: The congressman dropped out of the race because of insufficient funding and he reminded us that money is the mother's milk of politics.

9. **Never discuss politics or religion** an apocryphal saying that has been passed on for generations. Both politics and religion are topics that can cause intense disagreement or conflicts

Example: Most work places have a policy against discussing politics or religion.

10. **Power corrupts absolute power corrupts absolutely** Between 1837 and 1869 he was known as Sir John Dalberg-Acton, 8th Baronet. He is perhaps best known for the remark, "**Power** tends to **corrupt**, and **absolute power corrupts absolutely**. Great men are almost always bad men...", which he made in a letter to an Anglican bishop. https://en.wikipedia.org/wiki/John_Dalberg-Acton,_1st_Baron_Acton#

Example: Most people have a way of letting power get to their heads, hence the saying, power corrupts and absolute power corrupts absolutely.

11. **Patriotism is the last bastion of a scoundrel** Samuel Johnson the celebrated British man of letters, wrote these words meaning, when called to account for their wrong-doings and misdeeds often politicians will often give an insincere or worse dangerously misguided answer--that they did it because they felt it was their patriotic duty https://en.wikipedia.org/wiki/Political_views_of_Samuel_Johnson

Example: Some of our politicians use catchy slogans such as "make America great again," but in reality, they are only patriotic when it's convenient therefore, the saying: patriotism is the last bastion of a scoundrel is so true.

12. "**The buck stops here**" is a phrase that was popularized by U.S. President Harry S. Truman, who kept a sign with that phrase on his desk in the Oval Office. The phrase refers to the notion that the President has to make the decisions and accept the ultimate responsibility for those decisions. https://en.wikipedia.org › wiki › Buck-passing

Example: when someone says, The buck stops here shows that they are willing to be held accountable in the event that things don't turn out right.

13. **The ballot is stronger than the bullet** a quote that is attributed to President Abraham Lincoln.

Example: Democracy and going to vote are unstoppable because the ballot is stronger than the bullet.

14. **The pen is mightier than the sword.** The English words "The pen is mightier than the sword" were first written by novelist and playwright Edward Bulwer-Lytton in 1839, in his historical play Cardinal Richelieu. Richelieu, chief minister to King Louis XIII, discovers a plot to kill him, but as a priest he is unable to take up arms against his enemies.

https://www.bbc.com/news/magazine-30729480

Example: The pen is mightier than the sword, proves why freedom of the press is important in a democracy.

15. **the power of the purse** The influence that legislatures have over public policy because of their power to vote money for public purposes. The United States Congress must authorize the president's budget requests to fund agencies and programs of the executive branch.

Example: Most people can often be controlled by dangling a carrot on a stick in front of them, proving that the power of the purse is an important one.

16. **the road to hell is filled with good intentions** The road to hell is paved with good intentions is a proverb or aphorism. An alternative form is "Hell is full of good meanings, but heaven is full of good works"

Example: The thief said he intended to use his stolen loot to help the poor but he forgot to do so. The judge told him that the road to hell is filled with good intentions.

17. **to 'fall on your sword'** is, literally, to commit suicide or, figuratively, to offer your resignation.

Example: if your decision turns out to be a bad one, the damage might be irreversible and you will be fired hence, you will fall on your own sword.

18. **tilting at windmills** is an English idiom which means "attacking imaginary enemies", originating from Miguel de Cervantes' early 17th century novel Don Quixote and from the romantic, ill-thought-out actions of the story's hero of the same name.

Example: If you don't know what you are doing and you are not getting results it's like tilting at windmills.

19. **Trust but verify** The phrase became internationally known in English after Suzanne Massie, an American scholar, taught it to President Ronald Reagan, who used it on several occasions in the context of nuclear disarmament discussions with the Soviet Union.

Example: a good rule to live by when you don't know your adversary but you have to negotiate with them, then you should trust but verify.

20. **Uneasy lies the head that wears the crown** means that a person with great power, such as a king, is constantly apprehensive.

Example: Presidents are often busy and have lots to worry about, hence uneasy lies the head that wears the crown.

21. **When they go low we go high** At the 2016 Democratic National Convention, Michelle Obama first <u>uttered</u> her now-famous catchphrase, "When they go low, we go high" while discussing how to "handle bullies" in support of Hillary Clinton's bid for the White House. "Going low is easy, which is why people go to it," Obama said. "It's easy to go low. It's easy to lead by fear. It's easy to be divisive. It's easy to make people feel afraid.
https://www.okayplayer.com/news/michelle-obama-when-they-go-low-we-go-high-history.html

Example: When others hit you below the belt, you should be the better person and don't repay evil for evil; rather, show your class and dignity.

22. **You can't have your cake and eat it (too)** is a popular English idiomatic proverb or figure of speech. The proverb literally means "you cannot simultaneously retain your cake and eat it". Once the cake is eaten, it is gone. It can be used to say that one cannot have two incompatible things, or that one should not try to have more than is reasonable. The proverb's meaning is similar to the phrases "you can't have it both ways" and "you can't have the best of both worlds<u>."</u>
https://en.wikipedia.org/wiki/You_can%27t_have_your_cake_and_eat_it

Example: If you spend your salary on a Tesla, you can't afford, you won't have money for the essentials because you can't have your cake and eat it too.

23. **"Many of life's failures are people who did not realize how close they were to success when they gave up."**
-Thomas A. Edison

24. **"Success is not final; failure is not fatal It is the courage to continue that."**
-Winston S. Churchill

25. **"I find that the harder I work, the more luck I seem to have."**
-Thomas Jefferson

Part III:
25 Profiles of Awesome African American and Other Hosts and Guests from MSNBC, Fox News, and CNN, etc.

Stacey Abrams: Courageous, Unstoppable, Hero and a Legend

Stacey Abrams is an amazing and inspirational leader. She checks all the boxes as a black, minority, and woman. One cannot help but be impressed by her. Her signature "natural hair" is beautiful and the envy of many in both corporate America as well as in ordinary households because of its lack of pretense yet chic look.

Don't be disarmed by her youthful appearance and think you can underestimate her. Watching her speak, the way she handles herself in interviews lets the listener know that she is brilliant and in control. Stacey Abrams is also a writer and a published author, something most people might not know; and I just discovered it in the process of writing this book. This paragraph is from an interview in <u>The Atlantic</u>:

In addition to two nonfiction books—*Lead From the Outside* and *Our Time Is Now*—she has published nine works of fiction. Eight are romance novels, written under the pseudonym Selena Montgomery; her new political thriller, *While Justice Sleeps*, is the first novel to be released under her own name.

If Abrams is a skilled agitator and resetter of expectations, it is in large part because she has the capacity to imagine alternate realities, and the ability to bring the rest of us along. What's more, she understands this about herself. She's not self-aggrandizing, but she doesn't patronize with false humility, either. "I'm a good politician in part because I'm a very effective storyteller," she told me. "In my world, these are of a piece. I just deploy them in different ways."

https://www.theatlantic.com/magazine/archive/2021/06/stacey-abrams-novelist-while-justice-sleeps/618716/

From Wikipedia:

Stacey Yvonne Abrams (/ˈeɪbrəmz/; born December 9, 1973) is an American politician, lawyer, voting rights activist, and author who served in the Georgia House of Representatives from 2007 to 2017, serving as minority leader from 2011 to 2017. A member of the Democratic Party, Abrams founded Fair Fight Action, an organization to address voter suppression, in 2018. Her efforts have been widely credited with boosting voter turnout in Georgia, including in the 2020 presidential election, where Joe Biden won the state, and in Georgia's 2020–21 U.S. Senate election and special election, which gave Democrats control over the Senate. In 2021, Abrams was nominated for a Nobel Peace Prize for her efforts in the 2020 election.

Abrams was the Democratic nominee in the 2018 Georgia gubernatorial election, becoming the first African-American female major-party gubernatorial nominee in the United States. She lost and refused to formally concede to Brian Kemp in an election marked by accusations that Kemp engaged in voter suppression as Georgia secretary of state. In February 2019, Abrams became the first African-American woman to deliver a response to the State of the Union address .

https://en.wikipedia.org/wiki/Stacey_Abrams

Wolf Blitzer: The Most Empathetic and Sympathetic Man on CNN!

Wolf has the most interesting name on CNN and probably in the news media industry too! He has gone from a young Wolf to a fashionably gray Wolf with a beautifully trimmed silver beard and mustache! He is a constant visitor in my home at noon on CNN, the time that I watch his program. He has beautiful manners. He thanks his guests warmly when they appear on his show. They thank him back, and he says "thank you" again for extra measure. *What a nice man,* you think as you watch this exchange between Wolf and his guests.

His voice drips with concern and sympathy when discussing sad topics or bad topics! It is re-assuring to know that there are still nice people in the world like Wolf. You trust him with the news. You would probably trust him with your newborn or with your life! You would probably trust him more than your weatherman or woman since their forecast don't always pan out.

From Wikipedia:

Wolf Isaac Blitzer (born March 22, 1948) is an American journalist, television news anchor and author who has been a CNN reporter since 1990, and is currently Principal Anchor at the network. He is the host of *The Situation Room with Wolf Blitzer* and until 2021, served as the network's lead political anchor.

Blitzer has said he has frequently been asked about his name, which has been characterized as seemingly made for TV. He explained that his surname goes back for generations, and his first name, 'Wolf', is the same first name as that of his maternal grandfather.

Blitzer began his career in journalism in the early 1970s, in the Tel Aviv bureau of the Reuters news agency. In 1973, he caught the eye of *Jerusalem Post* editor Ari Rath, who hired Blitzer as a Washington correspondent for the English-language Israeli newspaper. Blitzer remained with the *Jerusalem Post* until 1990, covering both American politics and developments in the Middle East.

In 1985, Blitzer published his first book, *Between Washington and Jerusalem: A Reporter's Notebook* (Oxford University Press, 1985). The text outlined his personal development as a reporter, and the relations between the United States and Israel.

In 1986, he became known for his coverage of the arrest and trial of Jonathan Pollard, an American Jew who was charged with spying for Israel. Blitzer was the first journalist to interview Pollard, and he later wrote a book about the Pollard Affair titled *Territory of Lies*. In the book, Blitzer writes that Pollard contacted him because he had been reading Blitzer's byline for years, and because Blitzer "had apparently impressed him as someone who was sympathetic". Pollard also hoped that Blitzer would help him "reach the people of Israel, as well as the American Jewish community."

CNN has selected Blitzer to anchor their coverage of all U.S. presidential elections since 2004. Since August 8, 2005, Blitzer has hosted *The Situation Room*, a two-hour afternoon/early evening program on CNN.

Charles Blow: Great Debater and Powerful Advocate

This man loves a good debate! His eyes start flashing and his voice starts to rise as he makes his compelling arguments. He is tall with an athletic build like a basketball player or an African warrior or chief. He fights for equality and justice for his people, his black brothers and sisters. I have never seen him lose an argument on TV. If he were a boxer, he would deliver crushing blows to his opponent like a Mike Tyson.

Charles Blow is also acclaimed for his writings about the plight of blacks in America. Here is what professor Gates says about his work:

"In his provocative manifesto Charles Blow gives us one of the most thrilling experiences as readers: the challenge of imagining an alternate future. Writing in a long tradition of Black visionaries who've wrestled with the political implications of place and power, he exhorts African Americans to reconsider the possibilities of home against an historical backdrop of past migrations. Blow is one of our most penetrating thinkers and brilliant essayists, and in *The Devil You Know* he is putting it all on the line." -- Henry Louis Gates, Jr., Alphonse Fletcher University Professor, Harvard University

From Wikipedia

Charles McRay Blow (born August 11, 1970) is an American journalist, commentator, and op-ed columnist for *The New York Times*.

Blow was born and raised in Gibsland, Louisiana. He graduated *magna cum laude* from Grambling State University, with a bachelor's degree in mass communication.

As a student, he interned at the *Shreveport Times*, *News Journal*, and *The New York Times*, edited the student newspaper, the *Gramblinite*, and founded the now-defunct student magazine, *Razz*. He also served as president of Grambling State's chapter of Kappa Alpha Psi.

He headed the graphics department at *The New York Times* and was art director at *National Geographic*.

In April 2008, he began writing a column in *The New York Times*. His column had originally appeared biweekly on Saturdays. In May 2009, it became a weekly feature and appeared twice, weekly, in December 2012. As of May 2014, it appears every Monday and Thursday.

Blow often appears on CNN and MSNBC.

On February 22, 2012, Blow referred to presidential candidate Mitt Romney's "magic underwear", an apparent reference to the Temple Garment, in response to a comment by Romney about two parent households. The comment was criticized as insensitive to Mormons. In response, Romney joked that "I guess we're finding out for the first time that the media is somewhat biased. Blow later apologized.

In 2014, Blow published the book-length memoir entitled *Fire Shut Up In My Bones*.

In August 2016, while appearing on CNN with Donald Trump presidential campaign delegate Bruce Levell, Blow called Donald Trump a "bigot" and said that anyone who supported Trump is "a part of the bigotry itself." In response to the Central Park birdwatching incident Blow wrote an op-ed in which he said, "Specifically, I am enraged by white women weaponizing racial anxiety, using their white femininity to activate systems of white terror against black men. This has long been a power white women realized they had and that they exerted."

In 2021, Blow published *The Devil You Know: A Black Manifesto* in which he advocates people of color taking direct action by moving to states where they can build a political majority.

KEISHA LANCE BOTTOM

Keisha Lance Bottom: One of America's Beautiful and Favorite Mayors

Keisha Lance Bottom was arguably as popular as the governor of New York during the height of the coronavirus pandemic. Some people are blessed with smarts, good looks, or power but rarely with all three. She walked up to the podium in a news conference as confident and serene as a goddess. Her fashionable hair style and tailored suit made her look like a business CEO but she is more than that. She is the leader of the world-famous City of Atlanta. When she spoke, everyone listened to her charming and endearing southern-laced accent! Her words and her calm and poise held the audience transfixed as if listening to a beautiful mythical creature.

From Wikipedia:

Keisha Lance Bottoms (born January 18, 1970) is an American politician and lawyer who is the 60th mayor of Atlanta, Georgia. She was elected mayor in 2017. Before becoming mayor, she was a member of the Atlanta City Council, representing part of Southwest Atlanta. President Joe Biden nominated Bottoms as vice chair of civic engagement and voter protection at the DNC for the 2021–2025 term.

Bottoms was born in Atlanta, Georgia, on January 18, 1970, to Sylvia Robinson and R&B singer-songwriter Major Lance. She was raised in Atlanta and is a graduate of Frederick Douglass High School.

She earned a bachelor's degree in communications from Florida A&M University, concentrating in broadcast journalism. She earned a J.D. degree from Georgia State University College of Law in 1994. She is a member of Delta Sigma Theta Sorority, Inc.

Bottoms was a prosecutor and also represented children in juvenile court. In 2002, she became a magistrate judge in Atlanta. In 2008, she ran unsuccessfully for a judgeship on the Fulton Superior Court.

Bottoms was elected to the Atlanta City Council in 2009 and 2013, representing District 11 in southwest Atlanta. She served until 2017. She was concurrently the executive director of Atlanta Fulton County Recreation Authority starting in 2015.

https://en.wikipedia.org/wiki/Keisha_Lance_Bottoms

Laura Coates: Brilliant Scholar and Legal Mind

Don't let her youth and good looks fool you. She is always stylishly dressed and her makeup and hair effortlessly enhance her beauty. She might look like a prom queen or a beauty queen pageant winner, but her smarts are ten times that of most college quarterbacks and she is a proven winner. The words just come flowing out of her mouth like a lawyer or judge without a script. She is a real pleasure to look at and listen to on TV. It is no wonder that Alex Trebek from Jeopardy was impressed by her and chose her for consideration as a finalist to host "Jeopardy".

From Wikipedia:

Laura Gayle Coates (born July 11, 1980) is an American legal analyst for CNN. In May 2016 she joined CNN as a legal analyst. Since 2017, she has hosted a talk radio-show, *The Laura Coates Show*, on radio *SiriusXM's Urban View*. *The Laura Coates Show* moved to *SiriusXM's POTUS* early in January, 2021. Coates is an adjunct law professor at the George Washington University School of Law and routinely speaks across the country on civil rights, social justice, economic empowerment and other topics.

In July 2018, Coates was mentioned by *Jeopardy!* host Alex Trebek as a possible replacement once his contract was completed.

In 2001, Coates earned her bachelor's degree at the School of Public and International Affairs at Princeton University in New Jersey. In 2005, she received her *Juris Doctor* from the University of Minnesota Law School.

https://en.wikipedia.org/wiki/Laura_Coates

Anderson Cooper: Man-Handled the Pillow Guy!

Anderson leans his head and listens with compassion to his guests. His piercing blue eyes radiate warmth and love for everyone: environmentalists, CNN heroes, activists, Democrats, and Republicans. However, those who are anti-reporters, anti-democracy or con artists look out! He is movie star handsome with permanently grey hair since he was probably a teenager, and porcelain white skin. He is very athletic and is in peak physical shape.

I watched him take down the "My Pillow Guy" on TV because the latter made the mistake of under-estimating Anderson's preparation and bright mind. The My Pillow Guy was repeating a host of Trump talking points and lies. Anderson relentlessly asked him for facts and evidence, nailing him like a speared fish. Pillow Guy appeared dazed, confused, and reduced to a blathering idiot on television during prime time!

From Wikipedia:

Anderson Hays Cooper (born June 3, 1967) is an American television journalist. He is the primary <u>anchor</u> of the <u>CNN</u> news broadcast show <u>*Anderson Cooper 360°*</u>. In addition to his duties at CNN, Cooper serves as a correspondent for <u>*60 Minutes*</u> on <u>CBS News</u>.

Born into a wealthy family in Manhattan, Cooper graduated from Yale University with a Bachelor of Arts in 1989. As a young journalist, he began traveling the world, shooting footage of war-torn regions for Channel One News. Cooper was hired by ABC News as a correspondent in 1995, but he soon took more jobs throughout the network, working for a short time as a co-anchor, reality game show host, and fill-in morning talk show host.

In 2001, Cooper joined CNN, where he was given his own show, *Anderson Cooper 360°*, in 2003; he has remained the show's host since. He developed a reputation for his on-the-ground reporting of breaking news events, with his coverage of Hurricane Katrina causing his popularity to sharply increase. For his coverage of the 2010 Haiti earthquake, Cooper received a National Order of Honour and Merit, the highest honor granted by the Haitian government. From September 2011 to May 2013, he also served as the host of his own syndicated daytime talk show, *Anderson Live*. Cooper has won 18 Emmy Awards and two Peabody Awards, as well as an Edward Murrow Award from the Overseas Press Club in 2011.

Cooper came out as gay in 2012, becoming "the most prominent openly gay journalist on American television" at the time, according to *The New York Times*. In 2016, Cooper became the first openly LGBT person to moderate a presidential debate, and he has received several awards from the LGBT rights organization GLAAD.

Cooper attended the Dalton School, a private co-educational university preparatory day school in the Upper East Side neighborhood of Manhattan. At age 17, after graduating from Dalton a semester early, Cooper traveled around Africa for several months on a "survival trip". He contracted malaria on the trip and was hospitalized in Kenya. Describing the experience, Cooper wrote "Africa was a place to forget and be forgotten in." Cooper attended Yale University, where he resided in Trumbull College. He was inducted into the Manuscript Society, majoring in political science and graduating with a Bachelor of Arts in 1989.

Chris Cuomo: Great Teacher and Lover of Humanity

Chris is a guy with charm and good looks. Who wouldn't want him as a friend? He loves his guests and is gracious even when he disagrees with them! However, he has a low tolerance for liars, scammers, and shmucks! He will call them out and make them wish the ground would swallow them up! He hates hypocrisy and dishonesty! Because he's usually the smartest in any room, his guests have learned to be on their best behavior and cut the crap! When Professor Chris Cuomo says, "Let's get after it," he means business like a surgeon prepping to do brain surgery transforming a brain dead to a "woke" individual!

From Wikipedia:

Christopher Charles Cuomo (/ˈkwoʊmoʊ/ *KWOH-moh*; born August 9, 1970) is an American television journalist, best known as the presenter of *Cuomo Prime Time*, a weeknight news analysis show on CNN. Cuomo is the brother of current New York Governor Andrew Cuomo and son of former New York Governor Mario Cuomo.

Cuomo has previously been the ABC News chief law and justice correspondent and the co-anchor for ABC's *20/20*, and before his current show, he was one of two co-anchors of the weekday edition of *New Day*, a three-hour morning news show, until May 2018.

Cuomo was born in the New York City borough of Queens. He is the youngest child of Mario Cuomo, the former Governor of New York, and Matilda Cuomo (née Raffa), and the brother of Andrew Cuomo, the current Governor of New York. His parents were both of Italian descent; his paternal grandparents were from Nocera Inferiore and Tramonti in the Campania region of southern Italy, while his maternal grandparents were from Sicily (his grandfather from Messina).

Cuomo was educated at Immaculate Conception School in Jamaica, Queens, and at The Albany Academy, a private university preparatory day school in Albany, New York, followed by Yale, where he earned an undergraduate degree, and Fordham, where he earned his Juris Doctor (J.D.) in 1995. He is a licensed attorney.

https://en.wikipedia.org/wiki/Chris_Cuomo

Michael Dyson: Powerful Professor and Advocate for Justice

I could listen to Professor Dyson talk all day long! He is an imposing man in height and academic stature and has gone from a young handsome Denzel Washington to an older handsome Smokey Robinson. He has the knowledge, expertise, and the words to analyze anything and serve it to you as easy as baby food. All the while, he is entertaining you and making your brain and your consciousness expand. What a treat it must be for his students to listen to his lectures and his ideas. We get to enjoy him for free on CNN and other stations. The professor is also a powerful man of God which is an extra blessing.

Someone has written about Michael Dyson's work:

"Michael Eric Dyson is one of the nation's most thoughtful and critical thinkers in social inequality and the demands of justice. *Long Time Coming*, his latest formidable, compelling book, has much to offer on our nation's crucial need for racial reckoning and the way forward."

From Wikipedia:

Michael Eric Dyson (born October 23, 1958) is an academic, author, ordained minister, and radio host. He is a professor in the College of Arts and Science and in the Divinity School at Vanderbilt University. Described by Michael A. Fletcher as "a Princeton Ph.D. and a child of the streets who takes pains never to separate the two", Dyson has authored or edited more than twenty books dealing with subjects such as Malcolm X, Martin Luther King Jr., Marvin Gaye, Barack Obama, *Illmatic* (Nas's debut album), Bill Cosby, Tupac Shakur and Hurricane Katrina.

Dyson was born on October 23, 1958, in Detroit, Michigan, the son of Addie Mae Leonard, who was from Alabama. He was adopted by his stepfather, Everett Dyson. He attended Cranbrook School in Bloomfield Hills, Michigan, on an academic scholarship but left and completed his education at Northwestern High School. He became an ordained Baptist minister at nineteen years of age. Having worked in factories in Detroit to support his family, he entered Knoxville College as a freshman at the age of twenty-one. Dyson received his bachelor's degree, *magna cum laude*, from Carson–Newman College in 1985. He received a Ph.D. in religion from Princeton University in 1993 after completing a doctoral dissertation titled *Uses of Heroes: Celebration and Criticism in the Interpretation of Malcolm X and Martin Luther King, Jr.*

en.wikipedia.org/wiki/Michael_Eric_Dyson

Joey Jackson: Super-lawyer, Smooth and Talented

There is a saying: If you have a good voice but not the looks, you should do radio; but if you are good looking and have a good voice, you should do television! This would apply to handsome super-lawyer Joey Jackson. If he appears in any courtroom, he has an immediate advantage for being a good looking intelligent black man like the Lebron James of the courtroom. He's capable of making the most convincing arguments as effortlessly as Lebron making 3- point shots and cruising to victory!

From Wikipedia:

Joey Jackson (born September 15, 1966) is an American criminal defense attorney with a practice based in New York City. The former NY state prosecutor is a legal analyst for CNN and HLN and frequently contributes to other local and national media outlets as an analyst and legal expert.

Jackson received a BA from SUNY Brockport, an MPA from SUNY Albany's Nelson A. Rockefeller College of Public Affairs & Policy in 1992, and later a JD from Maurice A. Deane School of Law at Hofstra University before being admitted to the New York State Bar Association (NYSBA). As a law student, Jackson served as editor for the Hofstra Labor and Employment Law Journal.

As a graduate and professional student, Jackson held internships with the New York State Education Department (NYSED) and New York Democratic Congressman Charles Rangel's office in Washington, D.C.. While pursuing his Master's Degree, Jackson served as a Legislative Analyst for the New York State Assembly Speaker. Jackson is a former adjunct professor at Monroe College (Bronx, New York).

https://en.wikipedia.org/wiki/Joey_Jackson_(attorney)

Derrick Johnson: A Wonderful Leader and Humanitarian

Derrick Johnson is a good man doing a good job for the NAACP.

He comes across as a very smart man and a good ambassador for this legendary civil rights organization. Handsome and well-dressed, he has the words to address civil rights, voting rights, and social justice in America, or the lack thereof, in some areas! He is a young warrior with the energy and passion of a young Mohammed Ali when he won the first heavy weight championship of the world!

David Gelles from the New York Times wrote: Derrick Johnson, the president and chief executive of the N.A.A.C.P., was on the phone with other civil rights leaders on Tuesday afternoon, discussing strategy for how to respond to different possible outcomes in the trial of Derek Chauvin, the police officer charged with murdering George Floyd.

But before they could finish, news came that the jury in Minnesota had reached a verdict. Mr. Johnson and the others dropped off the call and waited. An hour later, the judge pronounced Mr. Chauvin guilty on the three charges he faced, including second-degree murder.

"When it got to the third guilty, I had a sigh of relief," Mr. Johnson said. "Because if the verdict would have happened differently, the energy could have been harsh."

Mr. Johnson finds himself at the helm of the National Association for the Advancement of Colored People, the country's foremost civil rights organization, when the nation is gripped by the most intense and sustained reckoning over racial justice in generations. It is a role that requires a versatile skill set. He sued

President Donald J. Trump in 2017 over the fate of the Dreamers, and again this year over the Capitol riot. He has walked the streets with protesters in Minneapolis and, before President Biden was inaugurated, pressed him to create a civil rights envoy in the West Wing.

https://www.nytimes.com/2021/04/23/business/corner-office-derrick-johnson-naacp.html

From Wikipedia:

Derrick Johnson is an American lawyer and humanitarian. He serves as the 19th President and CEO of the NAACP. He had previously served as president of its Mississippi state chapter, and vice chairman of its board of directors. Johnson is the founder of the Mississippi nonprofit group One Voice Inc., which aims to improve quality of life for African Americans through public engagement.

Johnson was born in Detroit. He attended Tougaloo College, then studied law at the South Texas College of Law, where he was awarded his JD.

https://en.wikipedia.org/wiki/Derrick_Johnson_(activist)

Van Jones: Brilliant and Dynamic Advocate and Teacher

Van is a man on a mission! As the saying goes, "He could charm the leaves off a tree!" Bespectacled and handsome with a neat Colonel Sanders goatee, he makes for compelling television because of his superior intellect. He is a racist's worse nightmare who shatters all the stereotypes of a black man not being able to speak as articulately, or to be as smart, or to be as hard working, or as successful as a Caucasian or any other member of another race. Van loves the black race so much that he cried on national TV. He was asked what it meant to him to have Kamala Harris become the first woman of president to be elected vice president of the United States. With the tears streaming down his handsome face, he explained the significance of the moment on a personal, national, and global level.

I was crying at home while he cried on television. Our country, which has done many things wrong when it comes to race relations and the marginalization of blacks, did something right with this elections result. This makes us all better, and gives hope to every little girl who dreams of becoming president. One day their dream can become a reality too.

From Wikipedia:

Anthony Kapel "Van" Jones (born September 20, 1968) is an American news and political commentator, author, and lawyer. He is the co-founder of several non-profit organizations, a three-time *New York Times* bestselling author, a CNN host and contributor, and an Emmy Award winner.

Jones served as President Barack Obama's Special Advisor for Green Jobs in 2009 and a distinguished visiting fellow at Princeton

University. He founded or co-founded several non-profit organizations, including the Ella Baker Center for Human Rights, Color of Change, and the Dream Corps. The Dream Corps is a social justice accelerator that operates three advocacy initiatives: #cut50, #YesWeCode and Green for All.

Jones has hosted or co-hosted CNN shows including *Crossfire, The Messy Truth, The Van Jones Show* and *The Redemption Project with Van Jones*. He is the author of *The Green Collar Economy, Rebuild the Dream,* and *Beyond the Messy Truth*; all three books rank as *New York Times* bestsellers. He is the co-founder of Magic Labs Media LLC, a producer of the WEBBY Award-winning Messy Truth digital series and Emmy Award-winning *The Messy Truth VR Experience with Van Jones*. He is a regular CNN political commentator.

Jones worked with the Trump administration and members of Congress from both parties to pass a criminal justice reform effort known as the First Step Act. Jones is currently CEO of the REFORM Alliance, an initiative founded by Jay-Z and Meek Mill to transform the criminal justice system. He was also a longtime colleague of, and advisor to, musician Prince.

Anthony Kapel Jones and his twin sister Angela were born in Jackson, Tennessee, on September 20, 1968, to high school teacher Loretta Jean (née Kirkendoll) and middle school principal Willie Anthony Jones. His sister said that as a child, he was "the stereotypical geek—he just kind of lived up in his head a lot". Jones has said as a child he was "bookish and bizarre". His grandfather was a leader in the Christian Methodist Episcopal Church, and Jones sometimes accompanied him to religious conferences. He would sit all day listening to the adults "in these hot, sweaty black churches". Jones was born after the assassinations of President John F. Kennedy, Martin Luther King Jr., and Robert F. Kennedy, but as he learned about the men's work, he became devoted to them as heroic figures. He pinned photographs of the Kennedy brothers to a bulletin 11board in his room in the specially delineated "Kennedy Section". As a child, he matched his *Star Wars* action figures with Kennedy-era political figures; Luke Skywalker was John, Han Solo was Robert, and Lando Calrissian was Martin Luther King Jr.

Jones graduated from Jackson Central-Merry High School, a public high school in his hometown, in 1986. He earned his Bachelor of Science in communication and political science from the University of Tennessee at Martin (UT Martin). During this period, Jones also worked as an intern at *The Jackson Sun* (Tennessee), the *Shreveport Times* (Louisiana), and the Associated Press (Nashville bureau). He adopted the nickname "Van" when he was 17 and working at *The Jackson Sun.* At UT Martin, Jones helpe11d to launch and lead a number of independent, campus-based publications. They included the *Fourteenth Circle* (University of Tennessee), the *Periscope* (Vanderbilt University), the *New Alliance Project* (statewide in Tennessee), and the *Third Eye* (Nashville's African-American community). Jones later credited UT Martin for preparing him for a larger life.

Deciding against journalism, Jones moved to Connecticut to attend Yale Law School. In 1992, in the aftermath of the Rodney King beating and trial, he was among several law students selected by the Lawyers Committee for Human Rights, based in San Francisco, to serve as legal observers to the protests triggered by the verdict. King had been beaten by police officers in an incident caught on camera. Three of the officers were acquitted and the jury deadlocked on the verdict of the fourth officer. Jones and others were arrested during the protests, but the district attorney later dropped the charges against Jones.

Jones's activism was also spurred by seeing the deep racial inequality in New Haven, Connecticut, particularly in prosecution of drug use: "I was seeing kids at Yale do drugs and talk about it openly, and have nothing happen to them or, if anything, get sent to rehab ... And then I was seeing kids three blocks away, in the housing projects, doing the same drugs, in smaller amounts, go to prison." After graduating from law school with his juris doctor in 1993, Jones moved to San Francisco, and according to his own words, "trying to be a revolutionary". He became affiliated with many left activists, and co-founded a socialist collective called Standing Together to Organize a Revolutionary Movement (STORM). It protested against police brutality, held study groups on the theories of Marx and Lenin, and aspired to a multi-racial socialist utopia.

Don Lemon: Great Communicator and Deep Thinker

"Come on Y'all don't fall for the Okey Doke! " The handsome, young African American TV personality was at it again! His face going from a scowl to a smirk as he went after his favorite topic—hypocrisy in politics! He loved his audience and they worshipped him! Don can make you laugh or cry and can make you feel what he's feeling!

He loves America, but he knows that America hasn't always loved or treated black people fairly! His sarcasm and deadpan, both a part of his clever sense of humor, are hysterical. He lampoons his target, the phony or jackass of the day, and shakes his head sorrowfully. "Don't fall for the okey doke!" Then repeats for emphasis with his trademark smirk, "Don't fall for the okey doke people!"

From Wikipedia:

Don Lemon, Donald Carlton Lemon (born March 1, 1966) is an American television journalist. Born in Baton Rouge, Louisiana, he anchored weekend news programs on local television stations in Alabama and Pennsylvania during his early days as a journalist. Lemon then worked as a news correspondent for NBC on its programming, such as Today and NBC Nightly News, after which he joined CNN in 2006, also as a correspondent. He later achieved prominence as the presenter of CNN Tonight beginning in 2014. Lemon is also a recipient of an Edward R. Murrow Award and three regional Emmy Awards.

Don Lemon was born March 1, 1966, in Baton Rouge, Louisiana. He has Creole ancestry; his great-grandfather was of

French descent, in addition to African-American ancestry. He attended Baker High School, a public high school in the town of Baker in East Baton Rouge Parish. Lemon was voted class president during his senior year.

Lemon attended Louisiana State University and graduated from Brooklyn College in 1996, majoring in broadcast journalism. While at Brooklyn College, he interned at WNYW. He worked for Fox News affiliates in St. Louis and Chicago for several years, and was a correspondent for NBC affiliates in Philadelphia and Chicago. https://en.wikipedia.org/wiki/Don_Lemon

Ana Navarro: Genius, Funny, and Passionate

Ana Navarro is a genius as a political analyst and she is hilarious. I love her dearly. She is beautiful, and energetic, and always has tons to say, and she says it well. When she gets excited, she talks faster and hits harder. She lapses into Spanish, my favorite language beside English, without missing a beat.

When she is disgusted, she will tell the host or the audience or the world, "He is a shmuck, ese cabron es loco," she adds for emphasis." Who else could she possibly be talking about? I wonder if she would say something as nice as that about a certain Donald Trump? Some quotes attributed to her are:

"Trump wears more make up than any drag queen I ever saw."

"Today is about #GeorgeFloyd and it's about accountability. But I am also so glad, there is a compassionate President in the White House who is not a racist and doesn't fan the flames of division, but acknowledges the systemic racism in our country and commits to addressing it."

From Wikipedia:

Ana Navarro, Navarro was born into a wealthy land-owning family in Nicaragua. She is the daughter of Violeta Flores López and José Augusto Navarro Flores. She and her family moved to the United States in 1980 because of political turmoil, though her father stayed behind to continue to fight with the Contras against the Sandinista government. She later said that Ronald Reagan's support of the Contras made her a lifelong Republican. She attended the Carrollton School of the Sacred Heart, a private Catholic college preparatory day school for girls in Coconut Grove, Miami. Navarro earned a Bachelor's degree in Latin

American Studies and Political Science in 1993 from the University of Miami. In 1997, she earned her Juris Doctor from St. Thomas University School of Law.

During her first year in university, Navarro raised funds for the Contras.

Navarro has served in a number of Republican administrations, including the transition team for Florida Governor Jeb Bush in 1998. She also served as his Director of Immigration Policy. She served as the National Co-Chair of the Hispanic Advisory Council for John McCain in 2008 and Jon Huntsman Jr. in 2012.

In February 2014, she became a political commentator for ABC News. In addition, she is also a political commentator on CNN and CNN en Español. Navarro became a contributor on the ABC daytime talk show *The View* from July 2013 to August 2018. She joined the series as a weekly guest co-host on November 2, 2018. She received a Daytime Emmy Award nomination for Outstanding Informative Talk Show Host in 2020.

https://en.wikipedia.org/wiki/Ana_Navarro

Toluse Olorunnipa: Powerful, Compelling Communicator and Thinker

Toluse is a tall ruggedly handsome man with a deep voice. When he speaks the words flow and people listen because he knows his stuff. At home I'm listening and saying to myself, *that guy is frickin smart and amazing and he's young!* I have to pinch myself and say: "Is that a brotha that is so smart not only holding his own, but talking circles around the other guests on the panel? Well, go head on with your bad self, homie!"

From an interview:

What are the most significant dissatisfactions and challenges connected with your occupation?

"It is very tough, especially these days, to find out the truth when there is so much misinformation, which makes the public think that everything is false and there is no way to tell what the truth is. … That type of cynicism can be injected into politics by unscrupulous people, and it can be hard for journalists to operate in that environment. It is a constant struggle but a worthwhile fight."

https://www.stanforddaily.com/2020/04/27/alumni-advice-toluse-olorunnipa-08-washington-post-reporter-cnn-analyst/

From Wikipedia:

Toluse "Tolu" Olorunnipa (*Toe-Loo Oh-lo-roo-NEE-pa*; born December 21, 1986) is a Nigerian-American journalist and political commentator. He is the first reporter of native African and Nigerian descent to cover the White House.

Olorunnipa earned a Bachelor of Arts in Sociology and MSc from Stanford University. In college, Olorunnipa wrote for *The Stanford Daily*.

Olorunnipa writes for *The Washington Post* and is an analyst for CNN. He previously worked for Bloomberg News and *The Miami Herald*. His columns have been featured in *The Wall Street Journal*, *The Chicago Tribune*, *Bloomberg Businessweek*, *The Tampa Bay Times*, *The Seattle Times*, *The Nation*, and others. He has been featured as a panelist on *Washington Week* and *Face the Nation*, and frequently appears on CNN, MSNBC, CBS News, and C-SPAN as a political analyst.

https://en.wikipedia.org/wiki/Toluse_Olorunnipa

Evan Perez: Powerful, Analytic, and Relentless

Evan Perez came across my radar because I would always see him on CNN. *He is African American, young and smart,* I thought. Come to find out he is a black guy but not African American because his parents are from my hometown of Belize. I became more of a fan and followed his career from that moment with enormous pride. Because I belong to many groups on Facebook, I found out that one of my friends on social media was also connected to Evan. She was in fact a relative of his. I was curious about him and asked my contact person lots of questions: what part of Belize was he from? What type of a kid was he? How did someone from Belize get to work on CNN?

I posted about Evan on Facebook and my Belizean friends commented and congratulated each other that one of our tribe was on the world stage. We toasted to the young man's health and success. In my mind, he became my adopted son. We both have Spanish last names; mine is Palacio and his is Perez. I like to talk on social media through my posts; he likes to report on world events on CNN. Can you see the similarities and the imaginary bonds?

From Wikipedia:

Evan Perez is a CNN Senior Justice Correspondent based in the Washington, D.C. Bureau, reporting on legal, crime, and national security issues. He was born on July 1, 1970.

Perez principally covers the Russia investigation and helps lead the team that covers the Department of Justice. Most recently, Perez, along with CNN colleagues Jake Tapper, Carl Bernstein and Jim Sciutto, was awarded the White House Correspondence Association's

Merriman Smith Award in the broadcast category for their January 2017 report on how the intelligence community believed Russia had compromising information on then President-elect Trump.

Perez began his career in Miami reporter as a reporter for the Associated Press. He was born in Belize City, Belize and studied journalism at the University of South Florida, Tampa.

Perez began his career in Miami reporter as a reporter for the Associated Press. He was born in Belize City, Belize and studied journalism at the University of South Florida, Tampa.

https://www.cnn.com/profiles/evan-perez-profile

Abby Phillip: Young, Gifted, and Black

Abby is the hardest working woman on CNN, I think. She has gone from a rookie to a princess. Now she is a boss or a queen. Her brilliance was always there, but she had to pay her dues. Being so young, she had to earn the respect of the TV hosts and other guests. She would speak fast to get her points in when she would be on a panel with older, venerable reporters. She has blossomed from a rookie to a star able to hold court, serve, and even dominate, tennis speaking.

At home I would be watching the news and whenever Abby flashed across the screen to give a report or as a part of a panel, I would turn to my wife and say: Look our daughter is on TV. She was beautiful chocolate complexioned and brilliant; she represented us so well on TV, so of course, she was a part of our TV adopted family.

For one so young, she is an intellectual and is wise. She has literally grown up before our eyes on CNN, commenting on national issues and testing her knowledge and expertise against some of the best minds in the media. Abby is a Harvard graduate and an awesome role model for all of us. She epitomizes what young African Americans can do when given a fair chance. Abby asked President Trump if he was a racist. Trump's answer confirmed the answer to this question in the way he attacked Abby. This became the norm for Trump, it seems, when dealing with black reporters.

From Wikipedia:

Abigail Daniella "Abby" Phillip (born 25 November 1988) is an American journalist who works as a political correspondent and weekend anchor for CNN. She has appeared as a guest on *Washington Week* and C-SPAN.

Phillip, born 1988, is of Afro-Trinidadian descent. She was born in Virginia to June Phillip, now a realtor, and Carlos Phillip, a teacher and later an educational psychologist. She has five siblings. When she was a child, the family briefly moved back to Trinidad and Tobago and returned to the U.S. when she was nine years old.] Phillip grew up in Bowie, Maryland, and attended Bowie High School. In 2010, she graduated from Harvard University with a Bachelor of Arts in government, after originally intending to study premed. At Harvard, Phillip wrote for *The Harvard Crimson*.

Phillip joined CNN in 2017 and covered the Trump Administration. Before CNN, she worked at *The Washington Post* where her roles included national political reporting and general assignments. She also worked at ABC News, where she was an ABC News Fellow and digital reporter in New York City. Phillip began her journalism career as a White House reporter and blogger for *Politico* covering campaign finance issues and lobbying. She appears occasionally on *Washington Week* with Robert Costa on PBS.

Phillip co-moderated the seventh Democratic debate of the 2020 Democratic Party presidential primaries at Drake University on January 14, 2020. She was criticized for unfair treatment of Bernie Sanders in moderating the debate.

In 2020, she landed a deal with Flatiron Books for *The Dream Deferred*, a book she is writing about Reverend Jesse Jackson's run to become the 1988 Democratic presidential nominee.

On January 11, 2021, Phillip was announced to be the new anchor on *Inside Politics*, replacing John King on the Sunday morning version of the political talk show (John King continues to host on weekdays), starting, January 24th 2021. The show is called *Inside Politics Sunday With Abby Phillip*.

Phillip lives in Washington, D.C., with her husband, Marcus Richardson. Phillip and Richardson were married at the Larz

Anderson House in May 2018. The couple announced they were expecting their first child in 2021
https://en.wikipedia.org/wiki/Abby_Phillip

STACY PLASKETT

Stacy Plaskett: Brilliant, Powerful, Super-mind

Congresswoman Stacy Plaskett was one of the managers of the impeachment proceedings against the 45th president of the United States of America. She is a beautiful stately woman with a smooth, dark coffee complexion and a school principal's stern demeanor.

By all accounts she did an amazing job in her role in the case against the President of the United States. She stated at the impeachment hearing, which was televised world-wide, one reporter from Vogue Magazine, https://www.vogue.com/article/who-is-stacey-plaskett-trump-impeachment-manager-virgin-islands, wrote: "You can hear the mob calling for the death of the vice president of the United States," Plaskett said, adding that she was certain that if the rioters had found the vice president and the Speaker of the House, they would have killed them both. Charged Plaskett: "They did it because Donald Trump sent them on this mission....President Trump put a target on their backs, and his mob broke into the Capitol to hunt them down.

"Nancy? Oh, Nancy? Nancy, where are you, Nancy?" as they searched the halls of Congress for her office; and—perhaps most chillingly—congressional staffers racing to barricade themselves in a conference room, just seven minutes before the rioters arrived and started thrusting their bodies against the door, trying to break it down.

From Wikipedia:

Stacey Elizabeth Plaskett /ˈplæskɪt/ (born May 13, 1966) is an American politician, attorney, and commentator. She is a

Delegate to the United States House of Representatives from the United States Virgin Islands' at-large congressional district and is a member of the Democratic Party.

Plaskett has practiced law in New York City, Washington, D.C., and the U.S. Virgin Islands. She worked as a House manager during the second impeachment trial of Donald Trump, the first non-voting member of the House of Representatives to do so.

Plaskett was born on May 13, 1966, in Brooklyn, New York and grew up in the Bushwick, New York, housing projects. Her parents are both from Saint Croix, U.S. Virgin Islands; Her father was a New York City police officer and her mother a clerk in the court system. Her family regularly traveled to Saint Croix during her childhood, so she became familiar with island traditions and culture. Her parents' home in New York was often home for students and other recent migrants moving to the mainland from the Virgin Islands. Plaskett attended Brooklyn Friends (a Quaker school) and Grace Lutheran for elementary school. She was recruited by A Better Chance, Inc. a non-profit organization recruiting minority students to selective secondary schools. Plaskett was a student at the boarding school, Choate Rosemary Hall, where she was a varsity athlete and served as class president for several years.

Plaskett spent a term abroad in France during her enrollment at Choate. She often states that Choate awakened her commitment to public service and a deep sense of responsibility to others through the biblical verse "to whom much is given; much is required". She was one of the few black students while she attended the school. In 1988 she graduated with a degree in History and Diplomacy from the Edmund A. Walsh School of Foreign Service at Georgetown University, where she was accepted under the early decision program.

Plaskett ran for student government at Georgetown under a progressive student ticket and was very active in the Anti-Apartheid Movement. As a student she spoke on behalf of universities in the DC area at the General Assembly of the United Nations. She received her J.D. degree from American University Washington College of Law in 1994. Plaskett attended law school at night while she worked full-time during the day with the lobbying arm of the American Medical Association and then with the law firm, Jones Day. In law school she studied constitutional law under her future colleague Representative Jamie Raskin of Maryland.

https://en.wikipedia.org/wiki/Stacey_Plaskett

Charles Ramsey: Thoughtful, Handsome, Great Analyst

If not America's favorite Police chief, he certainly is CNN's with good reason. This top cop has lots of knowledge and experience. From being a cop walking a beat, he rose through the ranks, achieving the coveted position of chief, an almost impossible rank to achieve for most black officers.

He is an imposing figure because of his knowledge and expertise as a police officer. He is a black man with light caramel complexion. The chief is handsome and is relatable to both blacks and whites; because he looks like both, not withstanding his neat afro hairstyle. He is a lighter complexion of the historic figure, Malcolm X, and he is just as good looking.

From Wikipedia:

Charles H. "Chuck" Ramsey (born 1950) is the former Commissioner of the Philadelphia Police Department. Prior to assuming that post in January 2008, he had served as Chief of the Metropolitan Police Department of the District of Columbia (MPDC) from 1998 to early 2007. In January 2017, he became a regular CNN contributor.

A native of Chicago, Illinois, he joined the Chicago Police Department as an 18-year-old cadet in 1968. After serving six years as a patrol officer, he was promoted to sergeant in 1977. He was appointed a lieutenant in 1984 and became captain in 1988. He served as Commander of the Narcotics Section from 1989 to 1992 before spending two years as a Deputy Chief of the police force's Patrol Division. In 1994, he was appointed Deputy Superintendent.

In 1998, he became the MPDC chief. During his tenure, he was involved in several high-profile cases as chief of police in

Washington, D.C., such as the Chandra Levy murder investigation. He has also been in the spotlight since the September 11 attacks focused attention on security issues around Washington, D.C.

Ramsey is a graduate of the FBI National Academy and holds undergraduate and graduate degrees from Lewis University in Romeoville, Illinois.

He has served as an adjunct professor at Lewis University and Northwestern University.

Ramsey is a former member of the National Infrastructure Advisory Council.

https://en.wikipedia.org/wiki/Charles_H._Ramsey

Joy Reid: A Bright Mind with a Beautiful Personality

Joy Reid is brilliant TV host. Young and energetic, she is passionate, fun, and engaging. She is a pleasure to listen to. She is good at holding the renegade Republican party accountable. She holds their feet to the fire for encouraging and enabling the previously twice-impeached and disgraced former one term-president.

From the "Daily Beast":

MSNBC host Joy Reid fired back at Tucker Carlson on Monday night after the Fox News star repeatedly labeled her the "race lady" in recent weeks, running down Carlson's past failures and controversies while claiming the conservative host was "making America worse."

Reid, who recently called Carlson a "male Karen" for urging viewers to call the cops on kids with masks, began her fiery takedown of Carlson by referencing that moment.

"At least three times in last month, Tucker Carlson took time off from badgering strangers in parks and bouncy houses to demand they show him their children's unmasked faces to refer to moi as the 'race lady'." Reid said. "'The race lady'? Why'd he call me that? I used to run track in high school but honestly, I'm not that fast. What else could it be? Hmm."

Reacting to a montage of Carlson running her down with that insult, Reid delivered a mini-biography of Carlson's personal and professional life.

"Did he say 'whitey'?!" Reid declared. "Oh, honey! Tuckums! Is this really about me fixating on race or is it about you fixating on race? I mean, when you recently went off on me for continuing to mask up post-vaccine while jogging in crowded Central Park, you weirdly threw in my attending Harvard. And I don't know, maybe I'm sensitive to this stuff, but it felt kind of like a dog whistle."

From there, she rhetorically asked Carlson if he had wanted to go to Harvard but was rejected, noting that while he probably thinks she was accepted because of "affirmative action," it was actually because she "had a really high GPA and fantastic SAT scores."

After saying Carlson's "girlfriend's daddy" helped get him into Trinity College and bringing up the recent controversy over his college yearbook, Reid then noted that Carlson was canceled by MSNBC and lost his CNN show after "Jon Stewart kind of humiliated" him. Baragona, Justin, "MSNBC's Joy Reid Fires Back After Tucker Carlson Calls Her the 'Race lady'" The Daily Beast, May 04, 2021.

https://www.thedailybeast.com/msnbcs-joy-reid-fires-back-after-tucker-carlson-calls-her-the-race-lady

From Wikipedia:

Joy-Ann M. Lomena-Reid (born December 8, 1968), known professionally as **Joy Reid**, is an American cable television host, MSNBC national correspondent, and liberal political commentator. In 2016, *The Hollywood Reporter* described her as one of the political pundits "who have been at the forefront of the cable-news conversations this election season." That same year, she wrote a book on the recent history of the Democratic Party, called *Fracture: Barack Obama, the Clintons, and the Racial Divide*. She hosted the weekly MSNBC morning show *AM Joy*, and in 2019 published the book, *The Man Who Sold America: Trump and the Unraveling of the American Story*. On July 9, 2020, MSNBC announced that Reid would host *The ReidOut*, a new Washington-based weeknight show in

Reid was born Joy-Ann Lomena in Brooklyn, New York. Her father was from the Democratic Republic of Congo, and her mother a college professor and nutritionist from Guyana; the couple met in graduate school at the University of Iowa in Iowa City. Reid was raised Methodist and has one sister and one brother. Her father was an engineer who was mostly absent from the family; her parents eventually divorced and her father returned to the Congo. She was raised mostly in Denver, Colorado, until the age of 17, when her mother died of breast cancer and she moved to Flatbush, Brooklyn, to live with an aunt. Reid graduated from Harvard University in 1991 with a concentration in the visual art and documentation form, film.

https://en.wikipedia.org/wiki/Joy_Reid

Susan Rice: An Encyclopedia of Information at Her Fingertips

Professor Rice? I don't know if she is or not, but she is a firecracker of an academician. Smart, brilliant, amazing brain are some words that would describe her. She is petite and pretty and her blackness is a beautiful, honey complexion. She has a computer like brain that spews out facts, figures, and data at a mile per minute. One of the things that makes America great is when we can tap into the genius of all our Americans regardless of race, creed, gender, or color.

With all its faults, America is still the greatest country on earth and is still the land of opportunity. A lady with an amazing trail blazing career of many firsts, she was even considered as a possible running mate for vice president for Joe Biden for his 2020 campaign. When I learned that she had written a memoir, I immediately bought a copy on the same day it was released, because of my admiration and esteem for this lady who has a long list of accomplishments.

From Wikipedia:

Susan Elizabeth Rice (born November 17, 1964) is an American diplomat, policy advisor, and public official serving as Director of the United States Domestic Policy Council since 2021. A member of the Democratic Party, Rice served as the 27th U.S. ambassador to the United Nations from 2009 to 2013 and as the 24th U.S. national security advisor from 2013 to 2017.

Rice was born in Washington, D.C., and attended Stanford University and New College, Oxford, where she was a Rhodes Scholar and received a DPhil (PhD). She served on President Bill Clinton's National Security Council staff from 1993 to 1997 and was the assistant secretary of state for African affairs at the State Department from 1997 to 2001. Appointed at age 32, Rice was at the time the youngest person to have served as a regional assistant secretary of state. Rice's tenure saw significant changes in U.S.–Africa policy, including the passage of the African Growth and Opportunity Act, support for democratic transitions in South Africa and Nigeria, and an increased U.S. focus on fighting HIV/AIDS.

A former Brookings Institution fellow, Rice served as a foreign policy advisor to Democratic presidential nominees Michael Dukakis, John Kerry, and Barack Obama. After Obama won the 2008 presidential election, Rice was nominated as Ambassador to the United Nations. The Senate confirmed her by unanimous consent on January 22, 2009. During her tenure at the United Nations, Rice championed a human rights and anti-poverty agenda, elevated climate change and LGBT and women's rights as global priorities, and committed the U.S. to agreements such as the Nuclear Non-Proliferation Treaty, Convention on the Rights of Persons with Disabilities, and the U.N. Millennium Development Goals. She also defended Israel at the Security Council, pushed for tough sanctions against Iran and North Korea, and advocated for U.S. and NATO intervention in Libya in 2011.

Angela Rye: Powerful, Passionate, and Brilliant

Angela is a very attractive and intelligent young woman who loves a good debate with a worthy debater. She appears often as a guest on television in regard to her work in social justice and or as a political adviser. She is a light skinned or complected black woman with a caramel complexion and the fine chiseled features of a model or a beauty queen. Listening to her is a thrill and a wonder at the same time: *How does she do that? How does she think so fast, how is she so brilliant?* Her opponent is given a chance to speak and, of course, he sounds like a racist male who is defending the indefensible. I'm thinking: *Oooh Angela is gonna get you good. Get him Angela!* Angela smiles but shakes her head in disagreement.

The host turns to Angela, "What do you think Angela?"

She starts slowly, patiently, lulling her opponent into a false sense of security. Then just like that she changes gears and lobs grenades and bombs and obliterates her opponent who has turned as red and deflated as a rotten tomato.

From Wikipedia:

Angela Rye (born October 26, 1979) is an American attorney and the Principal and CEO of IMPACT Strategies, a political advocacy firm in Washington, DC. She is a liberal political commentator on CNN and an NPR political analyst.

She served as the executive director and general counsel to the Congressional Black Caucus for the 112th Congress.

She currently is running the boards of the Congressional Black Caucus Institute, Congressional Black Caucus Political Action Committee, Seattle University School of Law Alumni, and Women in Entertainment Empowerment Network. She serves as a senior advisor to the Government Technology and Services Coalition and is a member of the Links, Incorporated.

Rye grew up in the Madrona section of Seattle, Washington. She graduated from Seattle's all-girls Holy Names Academy, the University of Washington, and Seattle University School of Law. Her father is Seattle community activist Eddie Rye, Jr. (born 1940).

Rye began her career in legislative advocacy at the National Association for Equal Opportunity in Higher Education, an umbrella association of 120 historically black colleges and universities in the United States. Here, she served as the Coordinator of Advocacy and Legislative Affairs. Prior to this, she worked in district office of Congresswoman Maxine Waters (D-CA) and served as the Western Region Director of the National Black Law Students Association.

Upon moving to Washington, DC, Rye co-founded IMPACT, an organization aiming to encourage young professionals in economic empowerment, civic engagement, and political involvement. Under her leadership, IMPACT formed critical partnerships with the National Bar Association, Congressional Black Caucus Foundation, National Urban League, Rainbow/PUSH, Congressional Black Caucus Political Education and Leadership Institute, Black Leadership Forum, and many other organizations. In 2013, Rye founded IMPACT Strategies, a political advocacy firm.

Rye is the only recurring guest on The Breakfast Club radio station. On December 6, 2016, Twitter users began championing her name to Charlamagne The God after he received backlash from tweeting he wished women of color had a platform "like Tomi Lahren did. This led to the two conversing and fostering a friendship they retain. In January 2017, she made her first appearance and since frequents the show almost quarterly to discuss updates on the Trump administration, current policy change, and other pop culture topics.

She also served as the Senior Advisor and Counsel to the House Committee on Homeland security, where she developed the general political strategy, focusing on modernizing government contracting practices and opening doors of opportunity for small businesses. She then served as the Executive Director and General Counsel to the Congressional Black Caucus for the 112th Congress. During her time as director, she was "tasked with developing the overall legislative and political strategy for the Caucus".

Rye is a political commentator for CNN and has been featured as an on-air personality on several media outlets, including *HuffPost Live*, TV One, and BET.

Rye has said that statues of George Washington and Thomas Jefferson, like those of Robert E. Lee, should be taken down because they were slave owners.

https://en.wikipedia.org/wiki/Angela_Rye

Bakari Sellers: The Youngest African American to be Elected to State Legislature

Bakari showed his brilliance for politics at an early age winning State office at age 22 in South Carolina. He is featured regularly as a guest on CNN for good reason. He is young, black, and handsome with matinee idol good looks. Dark coffee complexion like a strong rich brew, he exudes charm, confidence, and eloquence.

Bakari speaks with authority whenever he is invited as a guest on TV. He is an expert on social justice and the history of black folks in America. He can rattle off facts, dates, and connect the significance of the past to inform the future. He does so effortless and listening to him and learning from him is a joy as well as an education. One of his colleague's writes about Bakari's book, and this also has a bearing on his brilliance:

It takes a certain audacity to write a memoir before your 40th birthday, but Bakari Sellers is an old soul. Bakari carries scars from years before his birth; his father, a civil rights leader, was shot in the Orangeburg Massacre of 1968. Those shots still echo in Bakari's life. The youngest person ever elected to the South Carolina legislature, Sellers has always been a young man in a hurry. Bakari is my friend and CNN colleague, and yet this tale is filled with eye-popping anecdotes that I've never heard. I'm well aware of Bakari's gifts: political, legal, intellectual, oratorical. But I had no idea what a lyrical, beautiful writer he is. His voice is so strong, so fearless, so committed to the truth; the reader cannot help but be moved. My Vanishing Country is destined to join (dare I say it?) Dreams From My Father, North Toward Home, and even Stride Toward Freedom as an essential example of powerful personal testimony from astonishingly young writers. We need Bakari's voice and his vision now more than ever.

From Wikipedia:

Bakari T. Sellers (born September 18, 1984) is an American attorney, political commentator, and politician.

Sellers represented South Carolina's 90th district in the lower house of the state legislature from 2006 to 2014, becoming the youngest African American elected official in the country at age 22. He vacated his seat in the South Carolina House of Representatives to run for Lieutenant Governor in 2014, but lost to Henry McMaster. He was succeeded in the House by Justin T. Bamberg.

Sellers is currently a political analyst on CNN.

Sellers was born on September 18, 1984, and is the son of Gwendolyn Sellers and civil rights activist and professor Cleveland Sellers. He grew up in Bamberg County, South Carolina, and was educated at Orangeburg-Wilkinson High School, a public high school in Orangeburg, South Carolina. In 2005, Sellers earned a bachelor's degree in African-American Studies from Morehouse College, a private all-male and historically black, liberal arts college, in Atlanta, Georgia. In 2008, he earned a juris doctor from the University of South Carolina School of Law. Sellers has worked for Congressman James Clyburn and former Atlanta Mayor Shirley Franklin.

In 2010, *Time* magazine featured Sellers on its 40 Under 40 list. In 2012, *Politico* named Sellers on its "50 politicos to watch" list

Sellers was named HBCU Top 30 Under 30 in July 2014

In May 2020, Sellers released an autobiography, *My Vanishing Country*, that centers on the forgotten lives of African-American working class people in the rural U.S. South.

https://en.wikipedia.org/wiki/Bakari_Sellers

Tara Setmayer: Unparalleled Orator and Debater

Tara Setmayer came across my radar because of her energy, passion, and smarts on TV as a political analyst. She looks like an African American (But she doesn't have to be) with Anglo European features, such as her skin tone, which is like burnished gold. Her beautiful eyes are hazel, which match her complexion.

Doing this research, I found out that her father is originally from Guatemala. Maybe her dad's Guatemalan background explains her beautiful exotic appearance. Her mom is a Caucasian, so Tara may choose to identify with either side as her racial identity. She could also choose "other".

Tara Olivia Setmayer (born September 9, 1975) is a CNN political commentator, contributor to ABC News and former GOP Communications Director on Capitol Hill. She has appeared on ABC's *The View*, ABC's *Good Morning America*, and on HBO's *Real Time with Bill Maher*. On January 9, 2020, Setmayer was named as a Harvard Institute of Politics Spring 2020 Resident Fellow. Also in January 2020, she joined The Lincoln Project as a senior advisor. In 2017, Setmayer was named as a board director for Stand Up Republic, a non-profit organization formed in the wake of the 2016 election of Donald Trump to unite Americans behind the defense of democratic norms, ideals and institutions.

Prior to joining ABC, Setmayer was a CNN political commentator from 2014 through the 2016 presidential election cycle, regularly appearing on CNN's *New Day*, *Erin Burnett OutFront*, *Anderson Cooper 360°* and *CNN Tonight with Don Lemon* news analysis shows, and through 2017 subsequently appeared on CNN political panels, where she was credited as an ABC News guest contributor. Setmayer rejoined CNN as a commentator in January 2018. She currently writes for *Cosmopolitan*, and has contributed to *The Daily Beast* and CNN.com. She has also guest-hosted on SiriusXM's Patriot and POTUS channels.

Setmayer is married and currently resides in the New York City area.

Setmayer served as a former research fellow and communications specialist for the Coalition on Urban Renewal & Education (CURE), a non-profit organization dealing with the impact of social policies on America's inner cities and the poor. She also served as a political trainer for GOPAC, a conservative organization specializing in educating, organizing and training grassroots Republicans intending to run for public office.

From 2006 to 2013, Setmayer worked in the U.S. House of Representatives as the Communications Director for Republican Representative Dana Rohrabacher of California, during which she handled immigration and federal law enforcement policy issues, and led the national effort to free Border Patrol Agents Ignacio Ramos and Jose Compean through a presidential commutation.

For over two years, Setmayer served as a community liaison advocating on a variety of issues including affordable housing and services for the chronically homeless and children in South Florida where she co-founded a faith based homeless program. She was a regular panelist on the women's issues program *To the Contrary* on PBS, and was featured in several local and national publications including *The Wall Street Journal*, *The Hill* newspaper where she was included in the publication's annual *50 Most Beautiful* list in 2010, and *Ebony* magazine, on terrestrial radio syndication and satellite, *News & Notes* and *Tell Me More* on NPR and XM Radio. As a media commentator, she has appeared on a range of television programs on CNN, CNN International, ABC, Fox News, MSNBC and HBO.

https://en.wikipedia.org/wiki/Tara_Setmayer

Al Sharpton: A Warrior for Justice with a Golden Tongue

Reverend Al Sharpton burst on the scene a few decades ago as a leader in the black community. He loves the black race and has been fighting against police brutality and injustice in the black community, leading many marches, protests, and demonstrations. He has been seeking equality for us first in New York and then throughout the country.

As a man of God and a lover of his people, he has endured and weathered criticism from many in the establishment. It is always a pleasure to hear this powerful man of God on Television because he is a voice for the voiceless. His voice is deep and strong. He speaks truth to power.

With his signature slicked back, silver streaked, pompadour hairstyle, he is easily recognizable. In his younger days, he was a big burly man. Over the years, he has lost a lot of weight. However, he is still a voice and a presence that has not diminished, and we owe him a debt of gratitude for his many victories for the human family, black community, the poor, and the oppressed.

From Wikipedia:

Alfred Charles Sharpton. (born October 3, 1954) is an American civil rights activist, Baptist minister, talk show host and politician. Sharpton is the founder of the National Action Network. In 2004, he was a candidate for the Democratic nomination for the U.S. presidential election. He hosts his own radio talk show, *Keepin' It Real*, and he makes regular guest appearances on cable news television. In 2011, he was named the host of MSNBC's

PoliticsNation, a nightly talk show. In 2015, the program was shifted to Sunday

What I do functionally is what Dr. King, Reverend Jackson and the movement are all about; but I learned manhood from James Brown. I always say that James Brown taught me how to be a man.

Alfred Charles Sharpton Jr. was born in the Brownsville neighborhood of Brooklyn, New York City, to Ada (née Richards) and Alfred Charles Sharpton Sr. The family has some Cherokee roots.[1] He preached his first sermon at the age of four and toured with gospel singer Mahalia Jackson.

In 1963, Sharpton's father left his wife to have a relationship with Sharpton's half-sister. Ada took a job as a maid, but her income was so low that the family qualified for welfare and had to move from middle class Hollis, Queens, to the public housing projects in the Brownsville neighborhood of Brooklyn.

Sharpton graduated from Samuel J. Tilden High School in Brooklyn, and attended Brooklyn College, dropping out after two years in 1975.[1] In 1972, he accepted the position of youth director for the presidential campaign of Congresswoman Shirley Chisholm. Between the years 1973 and 1980 Sharpton served as James Brown's tour manager.

Cornel West: Powerful Preacher, Professor, and Philosopher

Dr. West is a legend and hero to many for his work as a professor, philosopher, and an activist for social justice as well as African American rights. Listening to him on television is always a treat. He has been wearing the same semi wild afro hairstyle for decades. Now he is gray and grizzled but still a powerful presence.

In an interview, he is apt to say, " Yes ma brother," or "that's right ma sister." He is comfortable talking to anyone, a janitor or a judge with the same humility and give them the same respect. Love for humanity emanates from him, someone who cares deeply for all. He is proud of his African American speech pattern, homespun, folksy style. Some blacks have had to learn to code switch, speaking one way at home and another in the corporate setting or workplace in order to sound less black or to fit it. We have a dual identity, as some might call it.

From Wikipedia:

Cornel Ronald West (born June 2, 1953) is an American philosopher, political activist, social critic, and public intellectual. The grandson of a Baptist minister, West focuses on the role of race, gender, and class in American society and the means by which people act and react to their "radical conditionedness." A radical democrat and socialist, West draws intellectual contributions from multiple traditions, including Christianity, the black church, Marxism, neo pragmatism, and transcendentalism. Among his most influential books are *Race Matters* (1994) and *Democracy Matters* (2004).

West is an outspoken voice in left-wing politics in the United States. He has held professorships and fellowships at Harvard University, Dartmouth College, Princeton University, Yale

University, Pepperdine University, Union Theological Seminary, and the University of Paris during his career. He is also a frequent commentator on politics and social issues in many media outlets.

From 2010 through 2013, West co-hosted a radio program with Tavis Smiley, called *Smiley and West*. He has also been featured in several documentaries, and made appearances in Hollywood films such as *The Matrix Reloaded* and *The Matrix Revolutions*, providing commentary for both films. West has also made several spoken word and hip hop albums, and due to his work, has been named MTV's Artist of the Week. West co-hosts a podcast, The Tight Rope, with Tricia Rose. In 2020, he was listed by *Prospect* as the fourth-greatest thinker for the COVID-19 era.

West was born on June 2, 1953, in Tulsa, Oklahoma, and grew up in Sacramento, California, where he graduated from John F. Kennedy High School. His mother, Irene Rayshell (Bias), was a teacher and principal, and his father, Clifton Louis West Jr., was a general contractor for the Department of Defense. His grandfather, Clifton L. West Sr., was pastor of the Tulsa Metropolitan Baptist Church. Irene B. West Elementary School in Elk Grove, California, is named for his mother.

As a young man, West marched in civil rights demonstrations and organized protests demanding black studies courses at his high school, where he was student body president. He later wrote that, in his youth, he admired "the sincere black militancy of Malcolm X, the defiant rage of the Black Panther Party, and the livid black theology of James Cone."

In 1970, after graduation from high school, he enrolled at Harvard College and took classes from the philosophers Robert Nozick and Stanley Cavell. In 1973, West was graduated from Harvard *magna cum laude* in Near Eastern languages and civilization. He credits Harvard with exposing him to a broader range of ideas, influenced by his professors as well as the Black Panther Party. West says his Christianity prevented him from joining the BPP, instead choosing to work in local breakfast, prison, and church programs. After completing his undergraduate work at Harvard, West enrolled at Princeton University where he received a Doctor of Philosophy (PhD) degree in 1980, becoming the first African American to graduate from Princeton with a PhD degree in philosophy.

At Princeton, West was heavily influenced by Richard Rorty's neo pragmatism. Rorty remained a close friend and colleague of West's for many years following West's graduation. The title of West's dissertation was *Ethics, Historicism and the Marxist Tradition*, which was later revised and published under the title *The Ethical Dimensions of Marxist Thought*.

https://en.wikipedia.org/wiki/Cornel_West

Eliott Williams: Brilliant Legal Eagle, Energetic

Eliott Williams is a frequent guest on CNN to comment on legal or racial matters or both. How did one so young accomplish so much. It is a pleasure to listen to him. He's very well spoken with an analytical mind that allows him to paint a verbal picture for the listener.

At about 5 feet 11 he's regular build with a youthful good looks and charm, who would have fit comfortably playing Carlton Banks on the show, "Fresh Prince of Belair," opposite Will Smith. Carlton was the smooth, debonair, and handsome genius black kid with Republican values. On the show Carlton's dad was a super-lawyer, Uncle Phil. Eliott probably comes from middle class or upper-class background, I don't know.

Whatever his background, he has made it academically and professionally based on his superior intellect and verbal skills which make him a joy to listen to on TV. He makes a wonderful role model for black and other minority kids. Sports, athletics, or a career in music as a rapper or an RB artist are not the only avenues available to our upwardly mobile generation today.

Maxine Waters: A Queen for Her Race and for Justice

Maxine Waters affectionately known in the African Community as "Auntie Maxine" is a popular figure! President Obama, who was voted the most popular man in the world 10 consecutive times in a row, or something ridiculous like that, would probably not win if he ran against Auntie Maxine in her congressional district. She is striking woman, who always looks smartly dressed and chic and could probably have been model in her younger days. She has had a long and distinguished career in politics, but it all stemmed from a background of social work and love for people. This propelled her into a life of service for the underserved and under privileged. She has been underestimated by many at their peril. She keeps getting re-elected time after time. Auntie Max is battle tested and has led her fair share of protests against racism, poverty, and inequity of all types. During the Los Angeles riots that erupted after the police beating of an unarmed black man, Rodney King, Auntie Max's rallying cry was, "No justice no peace!"

From Wikipedia:

Maxine Moore Waters (née **Carr**, August 15, 1938) is an American politician serving as the U.S. Representative for California's 43rd congressional district since 1991. The district, numbered as the 29th district from 1991 to 1993 and as the 35th district from 1993 to 2013, includes much of southern Los Angeles, as well as portions of Gardena, Inglewood and Torrance.

A member of the Democratic Party, Waters is currently in her 15th term in the House. She is the most senior of the twelve black women currently serving in Congress, and she chaired the Congressional Black Caucus from 1997 to 1999. She is the second most senior member of the California congressional delegation after Nancy Pelosi. She is currently the chairwoman of the House Financial Services Committee.

Before becoming a U.S. Representative, Waters served in the California State Assembly, to which she was first elected in 1976. As an assemblywoman, she advocated divestment from South Africa's apartheid regime. In Congress, she has been an outspoken opponent of the Iraq War and has sharply criticized Republican Presidents George H. W. Bush, George W. Bush, and Donald Trump, as well as Democratic President Barack Obama.

Waters was included in *Time* magazine's *100 Most Influential People of 2018.*

Maxine Waters was born in 1938 in St. Louis, Missouri, the daughter of Remus Carr and Velma Lee (née Moore). The fifth of 13 children, Waters was raised by her single mother after her father left the family when Maxine was two. She graduated from Vashon High School in St. Louis before moving with her family to Los Angeles, California, in 1961. She worked in a garment factory and as a telephone operator before being hired as an assistant teacher with the Head Start program in Watts in 1966. Waters later enrolled at Los Angeles State College (now California State University, Los Angeles), where she received a bachelor's degree in sociology in 1971.

In 1973, Waters went to work as chief deputy to City Councilman David S. Cunningham, Jr., then was elected to the California State Assembly in 1976. While in the Assembly, she worked for the divestment of state pension funds from any businesses active in South Africa, a country then operating under the policy of apartheid, and helped pass legislation within the guidelines of the divestment campaign's Sullivan Principles.[9] She ascended to the position of Democratic Caucus Chair for the Assembly.

Upon the retirement of Augustus F. Hawkins in 1990, Waters was elected to the United States House of Representatives for California's 29th congressional district with over 79% of the popular vote. She has been reelected consistently from this district, renumbered as the 35th district in 1992 and as the 43rd in 2012, with at least 70 percent of the vote.

Waters has represented large parts of south-central Los Angeles and the Los Angeles coastal communities of Westchester and Playa Del Rey, as well as the cities of Torrance, Gardena, Hawthorne, Inglewood and Lawndale.

On July 29, 1994, Waters came to public attention when she repeatedly interrupted a speech by Peter King (R-NY). The presiding officer, Carrie Meek (D-FL), classed her behavior as "unruly and turbulent", and threatened to have the Sergeant at Arms present her with the Mace of the House of Representatives (the equivalent of a formal warning to desist). As of 2017, this is the most recent instance of the mace being employed for a disciplinary purpose. Waters was eventually suspended from the House for the rest of the day. The conflict with King stemmed from the previous day, when they had both been present at a House Banking Committee hearing on the Whitewater controversy. Waters felt King's questioning of Maggie Williams (Hillary Clinton's chief of staff) was too harsh, and they subsequently exchanged hostile words.

Waters was chair of the Congressional Black Caucus from 1997 to 1998. In 2005 Waters testified at the U.S. House Committee on Education and the Workforce hearings on "Enforcement of Federal Anti-Fraud Laws in For-Profit Education", highlighting the American College of Medical Technology as a "problem school" in her district. In 2006 she was involved in the debate over King Drew Medical Center. She criticized media coverage of the hospital and in 2006 Waters asked the Federal Communications Commission (FCC) to deny a waiver of the cross ownership ban, and hence license renewal for KTLA-TV, a station the *Los Angeles Times* owned. She said, "The *Los Angeles Times* has had an inordinate effect on public opinion and has used it to harm the local community in specific instances." She requested that the FCC force the paper to either sell its station or risk losing that station's broadcast rights. According to Broadcasting & Cable, the challenges raised "the specter of costly legal battles to defend station holdings... At a minimum, defending against one would cost tens of thousands of dollars in lawyers' fees and probably delay license renewal about three months". Waters' petition was ultimately unsuccessful. As a Democratic representative in Congress, Waters was a superdelegate to the 2008 Democratic National Convention. She endorsed Democratic U.S. Senator Hillary Clinton for the party's nomination in late January 2008, granting the New York Senator nationally recognized support that some suggested would "make big waves. Waters later switched her endorsement to U.S. Senator Barack Obama when his lead in the pledged delegate count became insurmountable on the final day of primary voting. In 2009 Waters had a confrontation with fellow Democratic congressman Dave Obey (WI) over an earmark in the United States House Committee on Appropriations. The funding request was for a public school employment training center in Los Angeles that was named after her. In 2011, Waters voted against the National Defense Authorization Act for Fiscal Year 2012, related to a controversial provision that allows the government and the military to detain American citizens and others indefinitely without trial.

With the retirement of Barney Frank (D-MA) in 2012, Waters became the ranking member of the House Financial Services Committee. On July 24, 2013, Waters voted in favor of Amendment 100 included in H.R. 2397 Department of Defense Appropriations Act of 2014. The amendment targeted domestic surveillance activities, specifically that of the National Security Agency, and if ultimately passed would have limited the flexibility of the NSA's interpretation of the law to collect sweeping data on U.S. citizens. Amendment 100 was rejected 217–205. On March 27, 2014, Waters introduced a discussion draft of the Housing Opportunities Move the Economy Forward Act of 2014 known as the Home Forward Act of 2014. A key provision of the bill includes the collection of 10 basis points for "every dollar outstanding mortgages collateralizing covered securities" estimated to be approximately $5 billion a year. These funds would be directed to three funds that support affordable housing initiatives, with 75% going to the National Housing trust fund. The National Housing Trust Fund will then provide block grants to states to be used primarily to build, preserve, rehabilitate, and operate rental housing that is affordable to the lowest income households, and groups including seniors, disabled persons and low-income workers. The National Housing Trust was enacted in

2008, but has yet to be funded. In 2009, Waters co-sponsored Rep. John Conyers' bill calling for reparations for slavery to be paid to black Americans.

For her tenure as the chairwoman of the House Financial Services Committee in the 116th Congress, Waters earned an "A" grade from the non-partisan Lugar Center's Congressional Oversight Hearing Index.

When south-central Los Angeles erupted in riots—in which 63 were killed—after the Rodney King verdict in 1992, Waters gained national attention when she led a chant of "No justice, no peace" at a rally in the midst of the riot. She also "helped deliver relief supplies in Watts and demanded the resumption of vital services". Waters described the riots as a rebellion, saying "If you call it a riot it sounds like it was just a bunch of crazy people who went out and did bad things for no reason. I maintain it was somewhat understandable, if not acceptable. In her view, the violence was "a spontaneous reaction to a lot of injustice." In regard to the looting of Korean-owned stores by local black residents, she said in an interview with KABC radio host Michael Jackson: "There were mothers who took this as an opportunity to take some milk, to take some bread, to take some shoes... They are not crooks."

Fareed Zacharia: One of the Best Minds on the Planet

Fareed is an expert on international relations/politics with lots of books and research under his belt. He is clearly a brilliant mind and a deep thinker. Because of his dark non- European Anglo good looks and charming accent, you might dismiss him casually out of prejudice or bias. Maybe you are an "America First" type of person and don't think that someone with an accent can tell you anything. Maybe you are a trump supporter who feels threatened by minorities or who looks down at minorities. How did a multi-millionaire fool everyday Americans into believing he was "just an ordinary guy" just like them and win the presidency? Fareed wanted to know. So, he did valuable research and shared his findings on national television. Hillary Clinton and the entire field of candidates tried to tell us. Trump was a con-man. He was a scam artist. He was a phony and a fraud. He was morally bankrupt. He had filed bankruptcy many times. Why didn't America listen?

Criminals in California are allowed three strikes before they are locked away for life. Trump seemed to have a litany of sins and shady dealings that would have prevented him from being elected dog catcher in an old TV Western town movie. So why did he rise on top of the heap and win the coveted spot, the presidency of the most powerful country on earth?

Yes, Fareed Zakaria wanted to know. A stunned, bruised and battered Hillary Clinton probably wanted to know. Barbers in their barbershops gnashed their teeth, most black barbers at least probably did! Hillary Clinton was described as the most qualified person ever to run for that office.

Feminists wanted to know. Trump had been caught on a hot mic saying that he had no problems grabbing women by the private part. The feminists were not happy with Trump's victory. Trump did not know how he had won. What a shocker what a stunner. Trump is known as a B.S. artist.

In his heart of heart, he knows this himself and relishes telling jokes, tales, lies and outright whoppers. This is fun for him. He mocks people using outlandish facial expressions not seen since most people were in third grade and he mimics voices and expressions better than a third-rate paid comedian. Fareed made an entire show and production to describe and explain one of the most incredible con jobs or heists in history—how a con-man fooled ordinary every day Americans into believing he was one of them and win the presidency.

From Wikipedia:

Fareed Rafiq Zakaria (/fəˈriːd zəˈkɑːriə/; born 20 January 1964) is an Indian-American journalist, political commentator, and author. He is the host of CNN's *Fareed Zakaria GPS* and writes a weekly paid column for *The Washington Post*. He has been a columnist for *Newsweek*, editor of *Newsweek International*, and an editor at large of *Time*.

Zakaria was born in Bombay (present-day Mumbai), India, to a Konkani Muslim family. His father, Rafiq Zakaria, was a politician associated with the Indian National Congress and an Islamic theologian. His mother, Fatima Zakaria, was his father's second wife. She was for a time the editor of the *Sunday Times of India*.

Zakaria attended the Cathedral and John Connon School in Mumbai. He graduated with a Bachelor of Arts from Yale University in 1986, where he was president of the Yale Political Union, editor in chief of the *Yale Political Monthly*, a member of the Scroll and Key society, and a member of the Party of the Right. He later gained a PhD in government from Harvard University in 1993, where he studied under Samuel P. Huntington and Stanley Hoffmann, as well as international relations theorist Robert Keohane.

After directing a research project on American foreign policy at Harvard, Zakaria became the managing editor of *Foreign Affairs* in 1992, at the age of 28. Under his guidance, the magazine was redesigned and moved from a quarterly to a bimonthly schedule. He served as an adjunct professor at Columbia University, where he taught a seminar on international relations. In October 2000, he was named editor of *Newsweek International*, and became a weekly columnist for *Newsweek*. In August 2010 he moved to *Time* to serve as editor at-large and columnist. He writes a weekly column for *The Washington Post* and is a contributing editor for the Atlantic Media group, which includes *The Atlantic Monthly*.

He has published on a variety of subjects for *The New York Times*, *The Wall Street Journal*, *The New Yorker*, *The New Republic*. For a brief period, he was a wine columnist for the web magazine *Slate*, with the pseudonym of George Saintsbury, after the English writer.

Zakaria is the author of *From Wealth to Power: The Unusual Origins of America's World Role* (Princeton, 1998), *The Future of Freedom* (Norton, 2003), *The Post-American World* (2008), and *In Defense of a Liberal Education* (Norton, 2015). He co-edited *The American Encounter: The United States and the Making of the Modern World* (Basic Books) with James F. Hoge Jr. His last three books have both been New York Times bestsellers and The Future of Freedom and The Post American World have both been translated into more than 25 languages. In 2011 an updated and expanded edition of *The Post-American World* ("Release 2.0") was published.

Zakaria was a news analyst with ABC's *This Week with George Stephanopoulos* (2002–2007) where he was a member of the Sunday morning roundtable. He hosted the weekly TV news show, *Foreign Exchange with Fareed Zakaria* on PBS (2005–08). His weekly show, *Fareed Zakaria GPS* (*Global Public Square*), premiered on CNN in June 2008. It airs twice weekly in the United States and four times weekly on CNN International, reaching over 200 million homes. It celebrated its 10th anniversary on 5 June 2018, as announced on the weekly foreign affairs show on CNN.

In 2013, he became one of the producers for the HBO series *Vice*, for which he serves as a consultant.

Zakaria, a member of the Berggruen Institute, additionally features as an interlocutor for the annual Berggruen Prize.

Zakaria self-identifies as a "centrist", though he has been described variously as a political liberal, a conservative, a moderate,[1] or a radical centrist. George Stephanopoulos said of him in 2003, "He's so well versed in politics, and he can't be pigeonholed. I can't be sure whenever I turn to him where he's going to be coming from or what he's going to say." Zakaria wrote in February 2008 that "Conservatism grew powerful in the 1970s and 1980s because it proposed solutions appropriate to the problems of the age", adding that "a new world requires new thinking." He supported Barack Obama during the 2008 Democratic primary campaign and also for president. In January 2009 *Forbes* referred to Zakaria as one of the 25 most influential liberals in the American media. Zakaria has stated that he tries not to be devoted to any type of ideology, saying "I feel that's part of my job... which is not to pick sides but to explain what I think is happening on the ground. I can't say, 'This is my team and I'm going to root for them no matter what they do.'"

https://en.wikipedia.org/wiki/Fareed_Zakaria

Part IV

The Milieu:

The milieu, background, or setting that frame this book are: The pandemic, Trump's presidency, Joe Biden's election, the killing of George Floyd, and issues of racial reckoning. The year is 2020-2021. The world has been infected by the horrible Corona virus, Covid-19 which led to a global pandemic and a shutdown of most countries including the United States. The news cycles are dominated with stories of infection, death, and near death. Well over 500,000 people, many of them happy, thriving people, caught the virus and died within two weeks to a month. The hospitals were overwhelmed by the large amounts of people they had to treat.

In the beginning of the pandemic, many of them did not make it out of the hospitals alive. Then the mortuaries and funeral homes became stretched to the brink. Freezer trucks had to be employed to stack up the dead bodies to be buried at a later date. This same story was repeated in many countries. We were all in it together it seemed, at that time there was no vaccine for the dreaded virus. For those who caught it, their chance of dying was sometimes 50/50!

We are also just coming out of the Trump presidency, which saw our country become more divided and isolationist on the world stage. Trump seemed more interested in golfing and tweeting than addressing the ills of the country! He denied that there was a corona virus problem and was ineffectual towards it; until the virus spread like wildfire, devastating New York and then spreading to all 50 States and Hawaii. Trump the self-proclaimed deal maker was unable to bring Democrats and Republicans to make a deal provide a better universal affordable health care as he had promised. He failed to make a deal to reduce the supply of guns and hence reduce mass killings by active shooters.

In the last year of his presidency, he became consumed with his own re-election prospects and started to preach that the elections were rigged against him; even though, He had no evidence to support this outlandish claim. He ratcheted up his own attempts to prevent people from voting by calling the elections a sham. He refused to say publicly that he would concede to the winner if he should lose the elections.

His final act of infamy: he denied that Joe Biden won the elections and urged his supporters to go to the Capitol to fight the results of the elections. He was the orchestrator of the worst insurrection on US soil in over a hundred years. This led to at least six dead, scores injured, and a nation deeply traumatized by this assault on our democracy.

The Democrats have recaptured the White House and the Senate and are hoping to reverse President Trump's position on coal mining, other environmental unfriendly policies, strengthen universal health care, and improve social justice for under-represented minority groups.

Racial reckoning reaches the shore of Britain. Meghan Markle and Prince Harry have just revealed the reasons why they are at odds with Buckingham Palace. The Royal family is planning on seeking racial diversity training to adapt to a changing world and a more racially diverse population.

Part of the milieu of this book was the killing of George Perry Floyd in broad daylight. Officer Chauvin, sat on his neck for nine minutes effectively strangling him to death, all caught on camera and the footage was released for the world to see. The protests against police brutality were led by the Black Lives Matter group. Although in the middle of a pandemic, they marched and protested and rallied hundreds, thousands, at times, for many days and many nights. Their protests inspired people in other countries to follow suit in solidarity, proving again that our world is truly interconnected.

A Reckless President and the DC Riot

"Hi Magna," I said excitedly, answering the phone. I hadn't spoken to Magna for almost a year.

"How are you my beloved Cousin?" I inquired.

"Oh Frank, I have been in a deep funk since January 6th, the DC riots! I don't have energy to do anything! I can't even pick up the phone to make calls! I am stuck in the house watching CNN. I am hooked! There is always breaking news! Can you believe what has happened to our country because of Trump? Isn't it sad?"

I had to commiserate with my cousin. She had just borne her soul about Trump and she didn't even know or care if I was a supporter or admirer of the former president. As the saying says: never discuss religion or politics, especially if you don't know where people's loyalties are. She had just had it with Trump and needed an escape valve to get him off of her chest. We always did have a lot in common and got along well. We were both immigrants to California, teachers, and involved our Catholic Church ministries.

Now I was finding out that she was a CNN and news junkie just like me. She was the talker and I was the listener. I was ok with that because her stories were always interesting and entertaining. I would laugh and that would encourage her to launch from one topic to another. A phone call with Magna could easily last for two hours and was more enjoyable than a movie most times.

"I am like you, I love CNN and I could cry because of what trump has done to our country, Magna! I feel depressed like there has been a weight on my shoulders and in my heart. It's like we have been in a nightmare for four years because of trump! Thank God CNN is there to shed a light on all of Trump's antics, tricks and shenanigans."

And now my Cousin was mirroring almost exactly how I felt. How many millions of people felt the same way about the four years of Trump and the numerous "breaking news" alerts from CNN? Were they exhausted and overwhelmed and on the verge of cracking like a tortured prisoner behind the Iron Curtain like myself? Those almost daily alerts served to inform us, and at the same time, alert us about the crisis that our country was facing— the divisions (tribalism and cultural wars) the hurt, and the despair. Then there was the ultimate national shame, the day of infamy. A riot, a thing that was absolutely horrendous and unheard of, on the hallowed grounds of our Capitol, instigated by our own president, Donald J. Trump.

After talking to Magna, I felt as if a burdened or load had been lifted from my shoulders. I felt rejuvenated and re-energized. She always had that effect on me, I thought and I couldn't help smiling. It also reinforced the idea in my head that a book about CNN and the other major news network was worth writing about. It would be good therapy for myself and, who knows maybe for millions of others, who are experiencing the same exhaustion and inertia because of the direction that our country is going in.

As a part of the research for this book, I interviewed some of my friends and asked them, "What do you like about CNN?" Here are a couple of responses.

This is my Reason for watching CNN. With everything that has been going on in the world, I like to stay informed. I also get to see one of my favorites, CNN Senior Justice Correspondent, Evan Perez with Breaking New.... (Signed) Teresa

I love Cuomo. I always seem to agree with his assessment of the stuff that's going on today ... I have to tell you though, I just started listening and watching the news last year ... I also like Anderson Cooper ... His gentle manner can be mesmerizing at times. (Signed) Joan

Are You a "News" Junkie?

Do you love MSNBC, Fox News, or CNN? Are you a "news" junkie? Do you suffer from twitching, itching, or break out in hives if you can't watch the evening news for the first time in your life? Maybe your TV wasn't working, or you had another commitment. Friends came over and forced you to watch something else, so you missed the news and you felt out of sorts—like a fish out of water. Have you ever gone an entire day without deodorant? Uncomfortable right? Going without news is almost as bad as going without deodorant, right?

My definition of a news junkie would be someone who is obsessed with watching news. You must watch it as faithfully or as religiously or as compulsively as one, who for example, has to take a drink, exercise, diet, or check social media and so on.

My father, who was my biggest role model, was also faithful about watching the news. He worked hard sometimes two jobs to support his family of seven. Watching the news, from a kid's, perspective was one of his biggest joys in life.

"Turn off the music please. Let's turn to the news!"

I tried to protest, "But we listened to the news yesterday, dad."

"That was yesterday, my boy," dad said smiling. "News happens every day and I want to be informed and you should be informed too!" I had never won an argument with my dad. Our score card was Dad 100 me 0.

He was such a disciplined man. Growing up before television, came to Belize, my native country, I would watch dad listen to the news on the radio in English and then again in Spanish. By doing so, he also perfected his Spanish speaking skills. Due to my dad's influence, I followed his footsteps, and I grew to love both the news and the Spanish language.

Enter CNN: Breaking news flashes across the TV screen with all the bells and whistles, both visual and aural stimuli, causing us to respond like a kid rushing to the ice cream truck at the sound of the bells or horns outside. I guess CNN became the fix for a news junkie's addiction.

Words—their appeal, attraction, and their power:

Dr. Seuss probably had a "word" addiction, and so do I. Reverend Jesse Jackson, Reverend Al Sharpton, Maya Angelou probably have "word" addiction as well.

From as far back as I can remember, I have loved learning new words—the bigger the better! Hearing them, using them, and admiring those with the gift to write or to speak them, such as Martin Luther King Jr. did. Teachers and preachers, lawyers and TV and radio personalities who have this gift always inspire me. For this reason, I was inspired to become a teacher and writer, author and poet.

This book is about words, terms, sayings, and idioms. It is also about those articulate, brilliant minds that use them to paint a picture. They explain concepts and ideas in their roles as: news reporters, anchors, political analysts, professors, and the like. Words are fun and they have power. When you can understand the nuances and the different connotations of words, it can help identify you as being verbally gifted. Oftentimes there is a correlation with one's vocabulary and earning power.

This book is about the words and terms that are often used by the colorful hosts and personalities on MSNBC, Fox News, CNN, and even your local evening news on regular channels. Students, parents, and anyone who wants to improve their comprehension of these words, terms, and sayings may use this book as a resource. A side benefit of this book is that it can help their conversational skills as well.

CNN and the Black Community:

The black community loves CNN for most of the same reasons that the majority population does: their good solid reporting, hiring some of the best talent, and fair, balanced news coverage. For the black community, there was Bernard Shaw. He was a black host who was an original anchor on CNN, who did a great job and amassed a following and, as a result, was a revered figure and a role model.

Currently, there are probably more blacks as hosts and guests on CNN, who are very bright and highly educated, than on any other mainstream network. I have included my thoughts about their impact and influence on my life. I hope most of you, the readers, will agree with my assessment. I have included a bio sketch from Wikipedia of over twenty of my favorites, and hopefully, some of yours too. They are the epitome of brilliance, flair, dynamic personalities, and style. They bring a lot to the table, and I have learned a great deal, and I'm sure, so have their fans and the viewing audience.

I believe we all owe them a debt of gratitude. Many are leaders and experts in their fields: Mayors, Congressmen and women, political scientists, lawyers, judges, physicians, and so on. They are in a position to inspire many blacks and other minorities. Why does this matter? There was a time when the media was weaponized, (to use a CNN word), to work against blacks, portraying us as incompetents, criminals, or "less than". Clearly, due to better opportunities, changing times, more open-minded bosses, and in general a better milieu have all benefitted us as one family. Now blacks can be hosts, guests, and interview other bright black minds to counterbalance negative stereotypes of blacks. We are more than just athletes, entertainers, performers, or wisecracking, street smart, street talking people from the hood.

Who Gets What, When, and How

Politics and political science, as a conversation piece or field of study, borrows words, terms, and sayings from sociology, history, economics, and language arts just to mention a few disciplines. I observed while watching the news, for countless hours, that the words used on the news are interesting, new, and varied. The news seems to have a vocabulary of its own. The topics on the news whether local, national or international, are the driving force that created this new language. Hence, I came up with the idea for this book. I had to figure out and learn this new language.

Being a fairly intelligent person, as well as a teacher, I used my college background in English, economics, political science, and two years of law school, combined with my love for learning to understand the evening news. I decided to compile a list that would help any listener, who wants to improve or familiarize themselves with the words, terms, and sayings of the news so they can use them in context.

Politics is a fascinating topic because often people, both onlookers and participants, who are on opposite sides of an issue or debate may become excited or passionate about an issue. They become passionate! Some become so emotionally invested that they are ready to beg, borrow, steal, fight or even kill or die for their cause or beliefs. Politics invades or creeps into every aspect of our daily lives consciously, unconsciously, or even subconsciously. Face it, we are political beings. At home, at work, at church, or in the community, there are political decisions to be made. Who will lead, who will follow, who will lobby for the money, goods or services--things that the individual or group needs or wants.

Harold Lasswell, a famous writer and scholar, defined the study of politics as "Who gets what, when, how". In other words, picture the wealth or resources of a country. Who controls it and how is it distributed throughout the society? The type of government that exists in a country often determines how the wealth is distributed in a country. The United States is a free enterprise or capitalistic country and a person is free to make as much money as he or she is capable or wants to.

Most European countries have a socialistic type of government or a mixed economy that helps all of its citizens. They have more generous social programs by taxing their wealthiest citizens. The tax burden of their rich is much heavier than for our rich in the United States. On the other end of the spectrum, communism is a form of government where all the means of production are controlled by the government. Theirs is a supreme leader who is usually an autocrat or a dictator.

Importance of a Free Press in a Democracy:

America is a country that was founded on the belief that freedom was essential. Freedom from oppression, freedom of speech, and freedom of religion were all worth living and dying for. Our liberties should be enshrined in the constitution and that should be guarded and protected. People from all over the world come here seeking a better life, fleeing suppression and oppression, and once they land on our shores, they rarely go back to live in the country that they fled.

I came to this country from my native Belize, a small democratic country in Central America, as a naïve 20 yr. old, in order to attend a four-year college. I loved the freedoms that I enjoyed back in Belize. We have a stable government and two of our prime ministers have served three consecutive terms each, which speaks to the tranquility that we have there, unlike our neighboring countries such as Guatemala, El Salvador, and Honduras. We have never had a revolution, death squads, rigged elections, or political upheaval. As much as I love Belize, we have an entrenched two-party democratic system, and nepotism and corruption exists. Those who speak ill of the government, and their family, risk getting blacklisted from certain jobs; because those are reserved for the party stalwarts.

When I came to Los Angeles, California, I observed a level of freedom I did not know existed. Our freedom of speech allows ordinary citizens, politicians, television hosts, and satirists to speak freely and publicly without fear of death or intimidation. People can speak ill of the president, governor, mayor, or any other elected official without fear. I was shocked by this. I heard a radio talk show host refer to the, then, president as jerk, a moron, a racist and whatever else he could think of. I thought that was rude, offensive, and in Belize, would be very risky or career suicide.

I remember turning to my sister, Lily, and asked,

"Can't that DJ get arrested for talking so disrespectfully about the President?"

She laughed and said, "This is not Belize! People can say whatever they want! Nobody cares! This is America and we are free to criticize anyone we want!" My eyes must have widened in amazement and disbelief.

After having become a nationalized American and living here for almost forty years, I would bear arms and die for this country and for our freedoms and democracy that we enjoy. When Donald Trump came into office, I was willing to give him a fair chance and wish him all the luck in the world. After all, this is one of the few countries in the world where a man with no political experience, or record of benevolence, or love for humanity, can become president without guns, bombs, or military might.

Donald Trump started off by being unconventional. He even brought along his daughter and son-in-law as members of his inner circle, something unheard of before due their inexperience and the obvious issue of nepotism and conflicts of interest. Trump made very little effort to unite the country; rather, he ruled for his base who voted him in. He made sure we remained divided as Republicans, Democrats, and Independents. His approval rating hovered in the middle to upper thirty percent when he came into office and it remained the same for the duration of his term.

Another unconventional characteristic and constant of Trump's presidency, was his constant lying and spreading of misinformation and disinformation. His lies were often obvious and easily fact checked. For example, he claimed that the amount of people at his inauguration for president was larger than that of President Obama's; a lie he told the very next day after he became president. Trump became friends with autocrats and dictators such as the leaders of North Korea and Russia. Trump famously or infamously said, Vladimir Putin says he did not interfere with our elections." Seeming to favor Putin over our own American Intelligence FBI and CIA reports to the contrary.

As an American who loves this country deeply, I believe in our democracy. I furthermore believe in truth and honesty and integrity, and that those must come from our president. He or, she one day, should be held accountable and he should lead by example because what he says matters. He has a tremendous bully pulpit and a platform to influence people not only in our country but around the world. Truth must matter and America must matter. President Trump seemed to single out reporters to mock and ridicule and took ownership over the phrase "fake news," as a way to discredit the press who often uncover the truth about Trump's lies. Many politicians and dictators around the globe have watched the constant attacks on our freedoms and democracy in America, and whenever they are caught doing something wrong, they now lob the familiar defense, "Don't believe what you are seeing or hearing, it's all 'fake news'"! In his book, former Secretary of State, John Bolton, revealed that Trump said about journalists, "these people should be executed, they are scumbags."

Social Justice is Good Public Policy:

Some may ask, so it's debatable: Does white privilege explain the success of whites in this country? If white privilege did not exist would blacks and other minorities have equal access to good schools, jobs, housing, and justice in our courts? Is our racial and ethnic diversity in the United States our strength or our weakness? These are some questions that America must ask itself. As Americans, we should be asking them of ourselves and of others.

Our country, most people believe, is an experiment where different races have willingly come together to live, work, and co-exist in peace and harmony, and to unite and prosper as one nation. Some countries from the beginning of time were homogeneous in population such as: China, Japan, Korea, Russia, Germany, India, and so on.

Many believe that our country is now either at a turning point or a breaking point. America became the pre-eminent country in the world after World War II. Her growth and expansion continued fueled by her liberal immigration policies that sought and brought in some of the best minds: scientists, mathematicians, scholars, and highly skilled labor. They came from Africa, Asia, Europe etc. They also brought in cheap labor to work in fields, farms, and factories-- to do the work that the ordinary or average Americans won't do.

The new immigrants assimilated and chased after the "American Dream," placing heavy emphasis on a rigorous work ethic and a love for education, the so called, "key to success." Are there two types of justice in America? One for blacks and minorities and another for whites? The disturbing cases of unarmed black men being shot and killed by police officers would seem to suggest so. As a black person, I am in constant fear of crime in my community and then of crime against me by the police who are supposed to serve and protect.

The Black Lives Matter movement gathered momentum and strength, causing our country to consider issues such as: racial reckoning, social justice, police brutality, structural racism, voter suppression, and white privilege. The killing of George Floyd, an unarmed black man by a police officer who leisurely placed his knee on the man's neck—while the man pleaded for his life for nine minutes, was the final straw. This murder which occurred in broad daylight and in public truly shocked the conscience of the nation, and shocked the world. It definitely shocked those who were unaware of the separate justice towards blacks that exists in America—land of the free and, arguably, the greatest country on earth.

Young people are notorious for being impatient and full of restless energy. Black Lives Matter is a grassroots movement that tapped into this demographic. They were able to harness the power of social media to strategize and mobilize tens of thousands of young people to take to the streets to protest the killing of George Floyd and other black men who have died at the hands of police, in some cases, for little or no reason. Protests spread from city after city and then to other countries and continents.

We have to love our young people of all races who marched and protested for a better world. This is their world and their movement. They helped inspire celebrities such as Lebron James and his cohorts in the NBA and WNBA. Many other professional athletes from other sports helped spread the message of social justice. Many in the black establishment probably too old, cautious, or weary, were not at the forefront of these protests. They came on board later after our young people took matters into their own hands literally showing their absolute commitment and dedication and willingness to shed blood, sweat, and tears.

What is the connection between social justice and public policy? Public policy, according to Wikipedia, refers to laws which regulate behavior either to reinforce existing social expectations or to encourage constructive change, and laws are most likely to be effective when they are consistent with the most generally accepted societal norms and reflect the collective morality of the society. Society has a vested interest and a moral obligation to make sure that all the citizens in a country are treated fairly so that they can feel welcome, comfortable so they can have a sense of community and pride in their country in order to contribute and maximize their potential.

Think of a parent who has, for example, five children. If three are treated first class with love and affection and are given money privileges and benefits; but the other two are treated with constant physical abuse or neglect. Can you imagine the feeling of despair, futility, and rage that the two abandoned, mistreated kids would experience?

Social justice would require that a reckoning or adjustment should take place to right the wrongs and balance the situation, so that all five kids in this scenario would be treated better or equally. Public policy would say that it is in the best interest of everyone, and ultimately the state, that the five children should be treated equitably. This is necessary in order for them to become productive members of society and for them to feel valued and to have a sense of pride in themselves and their country.

In summary, from this illustration, the three that are being treated first class are the white establishment and the upper class which would include the wealthy of all races. The two children that are being treated shabbily would be blacks, Latinos, other people of color, and the poor who lack access to jobs, health care, and other basic necessities. Can most white people succeed and excel without the benefit of white privilege? Can most black people succeed without the benefit of affirmative action or quotas? Obviously, both are hypothetical questions. In a perfect world both social justice and public policy would ensure that people of all race and ethnicities would receive the same benefits and opportunities.

References:

1. Wikipedia
2. CNN
3. MSNBC
4. Fox News

Los Angeles, California News Channels
1. CBS 2
2. NBC 4
3. KTLA 5
4. KABC 7
5. KCAl 9
6. FOX 11

Dictionaries:

1. Dictionary.com | Meanings and Definitions of Words at ...

2. Dictionary by Merriam-Webster: America's most-trusted online ...

3. Urban dictionary

Acknowledgment

Special thanks goes to my wife, Glendarice Palacio, who has encouraged and supported this effort every step of the way. She handled and managed the household when I was
too busy doing research, writing, and numerous edits. Honey, I love you to the moon and back. Thanks Victoria and Justin and Jeremy for your prayers and feedback. Thanks to my dad, Ted Palacio, who made me watch the news as a child. My friends on social media, especially Teresa, Joan, and Cousin Magna, who are mentioned in this book, also deserve my thanks for always encouraging me.

I would like to thank CNN and their hosts and guests, especially those featured in this book, for their hard work and for the learning and education that I have gained from them. I am sure, I am not the only one who has benefitted tremendously from their gifts and talents. The same goes to the other networks such as MSNBC and Fox News; even though, I may not always agree with certain aspects of their news coverage.

Finally, thank you dear reader, for purchasing this book and encouraging your friends and relatives to do so. We are a village, and when one succeeds, we all succeed, so this book is dedicated to you, and will only go as far as we promote and tell others about it. You may always connect with me by email, at frankp2205@aol.com and through my website at www.frankpalacio.com, I would definitely appreciate your feedback.

About the Author

Frank Palacio is a prolific author and teacher at a public school in Los Angeles, California, a position he held for 23 years. He is a graduate of both California State University of Los Angeles, and Chapman University. He was awarded a Master of Arts Degree in Education. Frank was one of a select group of teachers chosen to attend the UCLA Writing Project as a fellow in 2005. Frank is also a musical composer, singer, and recorded artist. He is also a social media enthusiast and his posts have been liked, shared, and commented on over a million times. His work is available to peruse or download at www.frankpalacio.com.

Writing this book was a journey and an adventure because of the many interesting things that I learned in the process of doing research for the final product. I had to decide what to include and what to omit at each turn. Part of the challenge was to write a book that was more than just a dictionary of words and terms that are used on the news. I wanted to make the book more interactive and engaging by including profiles of famous people that the reader might have heard of so that there is a shared common experience; and if not, then the reader might want to read about their work and appreciate their talent, the way I have.

I particularly enjoyed writing the essay part of this book because it was cathartic. As a society we have been through a lot due to: protests, near civil unrest, pandemic, politics, racial reckoning, and on and on. We all deserve to hold ourselves accountable and even more so our politicians, for the type of country we would like to have or evolve into.

If you enjoyed this book, I have a hunch you would also enjoy some of the others that I have written. Please tell your friends about this book and explore the others: The books include:

1. Middle Schoolin: 50 Stories about the Humor, Rewards and Challenges of Teaching
2. Facebook Education From Middle School to Old School
3. President Obama: The Jacking Robinson President,
4. President Obama: 101 Likes, Moments, Similes, and More
5. Beautiful Belize: Interesting Words and Sayings
6. President Trump, Pinocchio, and Boy Who Cried Wolf.